The Art of Interfaith Spiritual Care

# The Art of Interfaith Spiritual Care

Integration of Spirituality in Health Care Regardless of Religion or Beliefs

Walter Blair Stratford

FOREWORD BY
Garth T. Read

WIPF & STOCK · Eugene, Oregon

THE ART OF INTERFAITH SPIRITUAL CARE
Integration of Spirituality in Health Care Regardless of Religion or Beliefs

Copyright © 2016 Walter Blair Stratford. All rights reserved. Except for brief quotations in critical publications or reviews, no part of this book may be reproduced in any manner without prior written permission from the publisher. Write: Permissions, Wipf and Stock Publishers, 199 W. 8th Ave., Suite 3, Eugene, OR 97401.

Scripture quotations are from the New Revised Standard Version Bible, copyright © 1989, Division of Christian Education of the National Council of the Churches of Christ in the United States of America. Used by permission. All rights reserved.

Wipf & Stock
An Imprint of Wipf and Stock Publishers
199 W. 8th Ave., Suite 3
Eugene, OR 97401

www.wipfandstock.com

PAPERBACK ISBN: 978-1-4982-9105-7
HARDCOVER ISBN: 978-1-4982-9107-1
EBOOK ISBN: 978-1-4982-9106-4

Manufactured in the U.S.A.

Contents

Foreword by Garth T. Read | vii
Preface | ix
Introduction | xi

Part 1: Interfaith—Acknowledging Differences | 1
    1.1. A Global Phenomenon | 3
    1.2. Fundamentalism and Mission | 13
    1.3. Abraham Is Our Father | 18
    1.4. Interfaith—Finding God | 23
    1.5. Hospitality in Dialogue among Difference | 28
    1.6. Habitat | 35

Part 2: Spiritual Care—Bridging the Differences | 41
    2.1. Dancing God | 43
    2.2. Tell Them *I Am* | 50
    2.3. On *Being*, and Meeting the Sacred | 56
    2.4. Listening | 61
    2.5. Meditation | 66
    2.6. Presence | 71

Contents

Part 3: Spirituality—Recipe and Ingredients | 77

    3.1. Imaging the Divine | 84

    3.2. Hope | 93

    3.3. Awe | 101

    3.4. Music/Painting | 107

    3.5. Imagination | 111

    3.6. Seeing into the Depths | 117

    3.7. Darkness Covered the Earth | 123

    3.8. Justice | 128

Part 4: Practicing the Art | 133

Bibliography | 139

Foreword

WALTER STRATFORD WRITES FROM the heart. This is not to suggest that this book is overly personal and that the tone of the prose is sentimental. Rather, it is to suggest that the book reflects the author's longstanding commitment to and passion for the two activities that together form the dual foci of this work. Throughout much of his professional life he has been engaged in pastoral care situations where people are being confronted by major personal challenges and are often experiencing deep trauma. At the same time, and intimately related to his public pastoral care work, Walter has maintained an appreciation of the realities of the multifaith nature of the local and global societies in which we all live. Multicultural and therefore multireligious awareness is an ever-present factor in the way in which he explores what he calls *The Art of Interfaith Spiritual Care*.

This is not a scholarly examination of the history and contemporary practice of either public pastoral care or interreligious relationships. Equally, it does not examine contrary views about the legitimacy of defining the human need and capacity to raise and answer questions about the "meaning of life," as *spiritual*. Walter's assumptions about this issue are made quite clear and, while acknowledging a range of different faith traditions, his personal Christian religious stance is acknowledged. Most of his illustrations are drawn from his personal adherence to and knowledge of the Abrahamic religious tradition and Christianity in particular. Readers wanting more detailed examples from other traditions are invited to consult other relevant sources.

As testified to in the Table of Contents, Walter has approached a very broad and challenging subject. To use one of his own metaphors, he has set before himself a large canvas on which to sketch the art of "spiritual

Foreword

care." As Walter suggests, works of art fulfil many different functions and can speak to a wide range of personal needs and situations. To pursue this image a little further, I believe that in this book Walter has filled in significant parts of the larger picture. More images and a greater range of colours would need to be added in order to claim that this is a comprehensive portrayal of spiritual care. Nonetheless, it reflects the hand of a competent craftsman and it has the ability to stimulate our interest in exploring further ideas about this and other aspects of pastoral care.

Throughout the book he merges (at times somewhat awkwardly) ideas about ways in which individuals might practice the art of personal spiritual care with ways in which carers (professional or otherwise) might integrate into their caring ministries some of the principles and practices that he is advocating.

The reading of this book will provide some fresh and intriguing insights into the idea of spiritual well-being. It may also stimulate further thought and enquiry among those seeking to enhance their ability to care for others who may be dealing with painful and traumatic experiences.

Garth T. Read, Coordinator

North Brisbane Interfaith Group
www.interfaithinaction.org.au

Preface

SPIRITUAL CARE, CONSIDERED BY many to be associated with an interventionist model, is in fact more aptly recognized in the presence of people, one to another. It is a process based on relationship and carried out in a climate of mutual trust. Religious affiliation is frequently a factor, but is not considered important in the collaborative work of finding meaning.

Relationships are always complex, even between friends who know each other well. Naturally enough this is exacerbated when we add together a multiplicity of faith standpoints and cultures. These are the factual, actual situations in which we all may find ourselves. What we do with these many differences in the lives of others, and in our own, depends on our understanding of who we are as people and the extent to which we are prepared to build the necessary relational bridges.

The pattern for this book therefore is shaped on a recognition that, while religious expressions differ markedly in their presentation, we can discern at the core of all religious expressions a supposition of sacred presence. It is therefore helpful for us all in the daily events of our life to approach people of other faiths with a degree of humility, recognizing that neither we nor they have a final answer to the question of faith. To facilitate our exploration into religious and relational complexities, I have divided the book into three parts. The three parts all belong together, and the separation here is for convenience and to allow for a closer examination of particular aspects.

Part 1 is an exploration of some of the complexities that emerge as we engage with other faiths, and makes clear the necessity of validating faiths within their own parameters. Comparisons are not helpful. Some of the complexity that emerges in interfaith engagement is found in the many instances of cultural differences that tend to be associated with differences in faith. This at times leads to the confusion of culture with faith. The two, while appearing to be connected, are not inseparably bound. It is important to differentiate between them, even while recognizing the degree of connectedness that they present.

Part 2, with the title "Spiritual Care," discusses ways for caring for each other in the search for meaning in which we all participate from time to time. Each faith's participation comes from an understanding of spirit presence, an understanding that is grounded in many years of adherence to particular religious beliefs and practices as the foundation for life. The varieties of faith standpoints are acknowledged as being true for their participants, each faith being recognized as having a valid place in the life of the earth.

Part 3 contains the claim that spirituality cannot be clearly defined. We are not able to look at spirituality in the same way one might look at a table. We are able to say that this is a table, and touch it and inspect it. We cannot say this of spirituality. It is not an object to be clearly visible. Spirituality has its own elements, however, and in describing these we can portray something of the essence of spirituality, and so envisage images that take us into the realm of spirit presence.

Part four focuses on some core understandings that must be considered in any practice of spiritual care. These include maintaining a close presence, valuing our common humanity, engaging in meaningful dialogue, practicing hospitality, and ensuring that safe habitats are established.

The fourfold structure of the book demonstrates the relationship in faith standpoints between understanding and practice, particularly the link between people and the sacred. The underlying assumption throughout the book is that all, in some way, are linked to that which is deemed sacred. This may take, for many, particular form in a religious standpoint, but this is not considered to be, as it were, a mandatory requirement.

Introduction

IN EVERY LAND WE find people who, in circumstances of loss, illness, disaster, and the like, discover a need to find someone who cares, not so much in a general sense, but in the context of a search for meaning. The thesis behind this book is that such care may be designated "spiritual care," and that spiritual care is the most apt way of meeting the needs that have arisen as a result of trauma of one kind or another. It is also necessary that in the active practice of spiritual care practitioners need to fulfill a threefold requirement. The body of the book seeks to establish the details of this threefold exploration as a means for understanding the ramifications of spiritual care. True spiritual care crosses religious and faith boundaries, and those engaging with others as interfaith spiritual carers will find this work helpful for the carrying out of their task effectively and with integrity amongst the complexities of interfaith interactions.

Firstly, we recognize that census figures confirm that over the last thirty years or so world population has increased considerably, and with that increase some increases in religious affiliation may be observed. Among religious bodies, Islam stands out as the one with the highest percentage increase. Given the spread of all religions around the world, it is clear that religious pluralism is a global phenomenon and therefore needs to be taken seriously. It is also increasingly important that in the mix of the *human family* all forms of religious expression are recognized and accepted as valid.

An important disturbing factor among all religious persuasions is the rise of fundamentalism, which needs attention as problematic in the life of the world. We will also become aware that, apart from any fundamentalist tendencies, all religions have a commitment to mission, and the expansion

Introduction

of their own sets of beliefs, a commitment that in its practice has the potential to sow seeds of discontent.

Christianity, Islam, and Judaism all claim a common heritage through the Abraham stories, but there is considerable variety in understanding this heritage. The elements of the story place Sarah as the mother of Isaac and the beginnings of the Jewish faith inheritance, and Hagar and Ishmael as primary figures in what became the faith of Islam. Christians, following the Jewish line and growing out of it with the elevation of Jesus, continue to acknowledge their faith foundations. If understanding is the goal, if there is to be any acceptance of different faith standpoints, a deeper exploration of the elements of another's faith is required. Most religious groups seek a relationship with a sacred other, and for many adherents this is a continuing search.

In the twenty-first century religions have reached a stage of being able to dialogue together, and we do well to remember that this needs to happen within the practice of hospitality. Dialogue has sought to understand the other's faith stance, even though there is some evidence of deep-down desires that others should have a faith more akin to our own. What is more important in the dialogue is the human connection, with each party having their own faith stance and each prepared to acknowledge the stances of each other as valid, but not needing to consider either their own or any other person's to be of more value. From all this it becomes important for all that diversity of faith be recognized, acknowledged as important, and validated accordingly.

As we progress, we will discover Buber's words "We are the dialogue" as a fundamental element in all dialogues. Dialogue also requires a degree of humility among participants. Dag Hammarskjold claims on our behalf that:

> Humility is just as much the opposite of self-abasement as it is of self-exaltation. To be humble is *not to make comparisons*. Secure in its reality, the self is neither better nor worse, bigger nor smaller, than anything else in the universe. It *is*—is nothing, yet at the same time one with everything. It is in this sense that humility is absolute self-effacement.[1]

Habitat, the locale in which we live, needs to be understood as having multiple associations. Not only is it our immediate place of residence, it is also the village, town, state, or country to which we have some allegiance.

---

1. Hammarskjold, *Markings*, 147.

Introduction

Habitat provides meaning, and a sense of normality in lives that may be fractured by physical and societal upheavals. More than anything else, the earth is the habitat for all people and must therefore be maintained as habitable.

Secondly, under the title "Spiritual Care," the book maps some of the more important parameters in the provision of pastoral care. As the chapters unfold, the reader is drawn into the imagery of a dancing God, and a place in the dialogue between Moses and God at the burning bush in the desert. This commentary also considers that, along with the story, a God with no name cannot be owned by anyone. This is in opposition to the mix of claims among Christians, Muslims, and Jews that the God they recognize can be identified, named, and located. Absolutist claims, however, are very difficult to sustain. The claims of these three major religious groups will become more acceptable among adherents of many faiths if boundaries can be softened, and allow for the possibility that the faiths of those many others are also valid expressions of the presence of the sacred in their lives. Indeed a more flexible approach to the divine in all religious standpoints may be considered a divine call, in the profound need for people to engage with each other as inhabitants of one earth. It is from the general understanding of spirit presence that spiritual care takes appropriate form. The reader will also be invited to consider some of the practicalities of spiritual care in listening, the practice of meditation, and the importance of presence.

Spiritual care, amidst the vast number of people in the world, considers the immediate interaction between two people to be the most important at the time. In unravelling difficulties—a primary activity in spiritual care—the world is not forgotten, nor are its peoples. Any search for meaning, however, is personal while continuing in the world. In this we may recognize the value of hope, which needs to be understood as a present reality, and as a way of life in which is contained the understanding that life must be lived. In the living we will come to understand that all aspects of life are of value, and should be valued as such.

Thirdly, to speak of spirituality is to speak of something that is most difficult to grasp. We can say that it has some connection with sacred things, but as a thing itself it is nebulous—unstructured. I have decided therefore not to endeavor to find a definition, but instead take us into a number of descriptive elements that make visible the variety of meanings that illuminate the essence of spirituality, and therefore the spiritual life. Contemplation of what our imaging of God means, of hope, standing in

Introduction

awe, imagination, the darker side of life, and more directs our attention to them as elements of life, each of which stands as a portrait of spirituality. Among these elements of life, justice stands out as a guiding force in the spiritual life. The prophet Micah draws our attention to some of the things we might want to offer to the Divine, and then straightens our thinking:

> With what shall I come before the Lord, and bow myself before God on high? Shall I come before him with burnt offerings . . . shall I give my firstborn for my transgression, the fruit of my body for the sin of my soul? He has told you, O mortal, what is good; and what does the Lord require of you but to do justice, and to love kindness, and to walk humbly with your God? (Micah 6:6–10, NRSV)

Fourthly, the chapter "Practicing the Art" is both a summing up and a reminder of the importance of our common humanity with all others. As human *beings*, we are required in the practice of spiritual care to be continually aware of individual value. Spiritual care emerges with human need and requires us to be hospitable. When people engage hospitably they begin to find safe habitats. Practicing the art of spiritual care involves dialogue and requires an investment of time and energy. We care for each other because this is what we are created to do, and although it may take us into unfamiliar territory we need to maintain an attentive presence.

Together these elements provide us with a resource that is essential for all those who would engage in spiritual care. Engaging in spiritual care clearly indicates the need to also engage with spirituality. Recognizing the forms that spirituality may take, we may also recognize the effect that Micah's call, for example, speaks to our own sense of justice. This may be particularly important in a pastoral interaction, more so when multifaith and multicultural issues are present.

While acknowledging my background as Christian, I would nevertheless claim that this book is of value among all those of any faith standpoint who lay claim to the value of spiritual care and the work of teasing out meanings in subsequent interactions.

PART ONE

Interfaith—Acknowledging Differences

THIS FIRST PART OF this book takes us into six aspects of interfaith. Religious experiences differ throughout the world, the difference frequently linked to culture. For centuries the world contained discrete groups, the association of these groups with others being remote or non-existent. We know little of their history apart from what has been discovered in archeological explorations. We know, for example, from these explorations that religion played an important part in their lives.

One of the peculiarities of religion has been the tendency to be associated with political aspirations in which religious forms have taken an active part. Dominant powers took their religion with them, imposing it on those whom they conquered. Ancient writings bear witness, and in the more recent *ancient* times, witness to the place of religion in the Roman Empire, and to the Greeks' Hellenizing influence on the people they ruled. Later Christian mission ventures swept aside both culture and religion in attempt to Christianize the world.

Christianity from its early days, in its understanding of God's presence in the person of Jesus Christ and the subsequent events of crucifixion, resurrection, and expectation of eternal life, considered the conversion of people of differing belief as justifiable. Early days for Christians were exciting but dangerous times, and raised strong expectations of the behavior required for salvation and eternal life. Such expectations spawned a strong missionary outreach which in time became an essential feature of the church. Difference was not considered favorably. In our day difference is widely recognized as a normal state of affairs, but is still for some

Part One: Interfaith—Acknowledging Differences

an aberration from true faith, and therefore necessitates making changes. Missionary outreach is still a strong motivation in many religious faith groups. Paradoxically, the Christian church itself is split into many denominations, some of which have nothing to do with others, yet all claim the Christian faith.

Religious and cultural differences abound and contribute to the richness and complexity of life in the world. It is most important that the differences are nurtured, and honoured, if we are all to live together in harmonious and just relationships. This first part of this book attempts to view some aspects of the differences found in the world in our day, in part with a view to raising awareness, and thus acceptance. The chapter headings are:

1.1   A Global Phenomenon

1.2   Fundamentalism and Mission

1.3   Abraham Is Our Father

1.4   Interfaith—Finding God

1.5   Hospitality in Dialogue among Difference

1.6   Habitat

When placed together, each of these aspects contributes to the picture of interactivity that I am seeking to draw. No matter what our faith and culture, a fundamental need in the world is that all get on with each other. There is no place for power and dominance in a world that is finite in all matters necessary for life.

1.1. A Global Phenomenon

Hans Kung, writing in *Christianity and the World Religions* (1985), provided comparative figures for the populations of world religions, taken from research results of the staff of the *World Christian Encyclopedia* (1982). Of the 4.8 billion people in the world at that time only 33 percent could be classified as lying within a Christian framework. Kung notes that "1.4 billion are nominally Christian—almost one third of the world's population. That compares with 723 million Muslims, 583 million Hindus, and 274 million Buddhists".[1]

In a comparison between these figures and more recent ones, there are considerable differences; one most obvious change is the increase in the world's population. This increase accounts for the increased numbers, but what is more helpful is the change in percentages. Figures from Worldometers for 2013 show the increase in numbers and also changes in percentages.[2] The world population in this year rose to around 6.9 billion. Of the religions referred to by Kung, Islam showed a substantial increase; the percentages of others show a lesser difference. In 2013 Christianity was 2.1 billion or 31 percent, Islam 1.6 billion or 23 percent, Hinduism 1.0 billion or 14 percent, and Buddhism 0.5 billion or 7 percent. Christianity, in these percentages, shows a slight decline. It is more important, however, that we take particular note of the questions posited by Kung in his response to the figures raised in his 1985 commentary, and the more recent figures that support and update his observations:

> Whether I am a Christian or a non-Christian, what is my attitude toward these other religions? That question is getting continually

---
1. Kung, *Christianity and the World's Religions*, xiii.
2. www.worldometers.info/world-population/

more urgent, since not only the geographical horizon of our religious world (thanks to the great voyages of discovery) but its historical horizon as well (thanks to modern history of religions) have expanded enormously. In a world so closely knit together, the old religious boundaries are becoming increasingly blurred; and we find large numbers of people with different faiths even in our own country in our home town, in our factories and schools, often on our own block. What indeed is my attitude toward these other religions?[3]

M. Thomas Thangaraj's essay "The Challenge of Religious Plurality," in *Plurality, Power and Mission*, reinforces Kung's observations, and calls us to think carefully about their implications:

> One does not have to travel hundreds and thousands of miles to meet a person of another religious faith. The people of other religions live next door to us. We meet them in the street, in the workplace, in shopping malls, and in other social and community events. This is becoming true of most places in the world today.[4]

"Interfaith" is a relatively new term coined in the realization that there is a massive global movement of people across borders into other countries. Right now, as a result of conflict, wave after wave are fleeing their homes. Many countries are experiencing a kind of invasion as poor people seek a better life, the displaced seek a permanent home, and the oppressed seek release and relief. All bring their culture and beliefs with them and, as aliens in the country into which they have entered, have considerable difficulty being accepted.

The two realities that face us in any exploration of interfaith considerations are, firstly, that the world's population continues to grow, and that growth changes the balance not only in religious affiliation, but also socially and culturally. Secondly, we live now in a heterogeneous society and can no longer pretend that we have some exclusive right to the place in which we live. The changes are particularly confronting Western society, affecting many countries that for centuries could point to the homogeneity of their social framework. In the Mediterranean, for example, large numbers of people make the hazardous journey in overcrowded boats from northern Africa in the effort to get to Europe. In these early years of the twenty-first century, as a result of sectarian and civil conflict engendering great fear

3. Kung, *Christianity and the World Religions*, xiii.
4. Thangaraj, "Challenge of Religious Plurality," 198.

1.1. A Global Phenomenon

in the populations of the countries involved, there is an unprecedented migration of men, women, and children from conflicted living to nations perceived to be places of order and peace. Thousands are on the march and the future of thousands more is flooded with uncertainty.

Indeed, the influx of refugees from countries of conflict has dramatically and irrevocably changed previously established social frameworks. The social and religious differences are in some instances quite profound. Refugees, almost by definition, come from impoverished circumstances, in fear for their lives because of political turbulence, and seeking a more peaceful and viable life. Colliding with a society that is different in many ways results in friction, which is at times severe. Asylum seekers stranded on the boundary between England and France are one example.

Perceptions of invasion by stealth have in Australia, and no doubt many other countries, led to restrictions imposed by governments that exacerbate the difficulties experienced by asylum seekers. Religious differences also have forced established institutions, particularly churches, to consider how the changes might be bridged, and interfaith conversations are an attempt to establish appropriate contact.

The word "interfaith," however, is problematic in that it can be a considerable barrier in relationships. Ordinarily, people engage with each other regularly, interactions occurring every day, establishing goodwill. The difficulties emerge within religious parameters, in rules laid down for adherents to follow when contacting others with a different denominational or faith outlook. This appears most strongly among religious evangelical and conservative expressions of faith and worship. Within all faith traditions, opposing groups have been recorded as denigrating each other to the extent of physical violence. It also becomes apparent in elements of religious bigotry across faith boundaries.

All have difficulty with interpersonal relationships. Race, culture, language, and history all impact the difficulties people have in accepting each other. All therefore have cultural clashes at times, and some of these clashes erupt into violent confrontations that involve large groups. Pockets of such violence have erupted in many countries throughout the world. Controlled by authority for now, suspicion and misunderstanding continues to bubble beneath the surface. Down the centuries, multiple forms of behavior and systems of belief and life have developed around the globe. The web that holds it all together is at times most fragile.

Part One: Interfaith—Acknowledging Differences

Part of the difficulty lies in the concept *God*, in particular that taken up by Christians and developed by the church. Christianity has its roots in Jewish religious culture, but also with an overlay of ancient understandings of the nature of the world. Taken from ancient times, when the world was flat with an inverted bowl over the top, heaven above the bowl was the dwelling place of the gods. These gods were perceived to be ruled by a God who was supreme. Elements of these myths can be found in many stories of ancient nations and groups. In Rome, families put their faith in family gods and daily rituals. In Greek mythology, Zeus was the god of the sky and ruler of the Olympian gods. The Hebrew scriptures also carry some of these mythical elements, which can be recognized in Psalms 82 ("God has taken his place in the divine council; in the midst of the gods he holds judgement") and 89 ("Who among the heavenly beings is like the Lord, a God feared in the council of the holy ones"), along with Job 1:6 ("One day the heavenly beings came to present themselves before the Lord") and Genesis 6:1–4("the sons of God saw that they [human girls] were fair; and they took wives for themselves"). Even the Christian creeds contain some of this character when they speak of Jesus seated at the right hand of God. Something of this notion of God is still carried within the dogma of the Christian church. Worship is directed towards God, who clearly is located somewhere else.

Similarly, this notion can be found in Judaism and Islam, so that something like half the world's population has this perception and is focused on a single divine figure. The other half of the world's population is comfortable with a plurality of god figures or none at all. Christianity and Islam are the most raucous in their claims of God's supremacy. Each has a different conception of God and the role of adherents, even though they both claim Abraham as their faith father figure, and thus claim Abraham's God as their own. Christianity and Islam have been the most aggressive over the centuries in their missionary activity.

Christian missionary activity, which has included an assumption of the supremacy of God over other deities, meant for many the total displacement of their religious life, a denial of the gods they had adhered to for centuries, and entry into a foreign religious framework that included behavior, dress, and food codes that were foreign to them. At times these religious codes were enforced.

The history of the gods is closely allied to the history of colonization. Faith, while offering support, strength, and meaning to many, falls short

1.1. A Global Phenomenon

when it is linked only to a particular religious standpoint. Refugee claims put great pressure on resources, and on the magnanimity of others. People with a particular faith standpoint frequently spend so much time and energy defending their faith against the faith of others that they neglect their humanity, and at times sink into darkness. Fairness and generosity are lost in the politically generated fear factor. The fear is of a different culture but also of a different religious expression. Many in Australia who never attend church or express any interest become fearful of those whose religious fervor is strong and visible.

Even as this is written, major changes continue in the world. There is no standing still in the world, with its many religious and cultural affiliations. Fundamentalist groups, while laying claim to Islam, are with considerable cruelty seeking to establish statehood for themselves and their belief claims, invading areas that have been the habitat of others and forcing retreat or behavioral change. This has a knock-on effect, as Muslims everywhere are treated with suspicion and at times subjected to harassment. Many feel the need to defend their faith stance in the face of such criticism and distrust.

The Christian church itself is well versed in the practice of faith defence, for within the broad boundaries that encompass Christianity differences abound and are still hotly debated. History bears witness that for centuries people have been cruelly dealt with by and within the church when they dared to hold views that differed from that which was considered the norm. John Hick, however, writing of Christianity's history of absolutist claims, offers windows of hope as he makes the point that changes have emerged during the twentieth century, leading to some recognition of value in other religions: "The immense spiritual riches of Judaism and Islam, of Hinduism, Buddhism, and Sikhism, of Confucianism and Taoism and African primal religion have tended to erode the plausibility of the old Christian exclusivism."[5] Much of the spiritual riches referred to by Hick predate Christianity by millennia. Any consideration of them as baseless denies the validity of the religious life of believers who have found meaning for their lives. Being able to accept and then seek to understand these riches is one of the keys to genuine interfaith connectivity.

We cannot continue to proclaim the superiority of our own religious standpoint without alienating others. Clearly the burning question for all is: What indeed is my attitude to other religions? Within the wider parameters

---

5. Hick, *Myth of Christian Uniqueness*, 17.

Part One: Interfaith—Acknowledging Differences

of Christianity, however, one can still find exclusivism within the Christian framework, let alone venturing into the uncharted waters of other faiths. Spiritual riches are often tainted by attitudes. Among many Christians the *real* God begins with Jesus, resulting in a discounting of earlier religious experience. Some credence is given to the God of the Jews, frequently in the sense of a pointing forward to the fulfillment of prophecy.

Many Christians still consider the Old Testament as the forerunner of the more fulfilling story in the New Testament. The very notion of Old and New Testaments makes the point. Interfaith is indeed problematic in the face of groups determined to maintain the faith of ages without regard for the needs of twenty-first century life, in particular the threat of global warming and its possible consequences for all. Interfaith, lauded today as a great step forward in understanding between people of differing religious persuasions, in many ways mirrors the ecumenical movement in the early twentieth century. In that movement interdenominational understanding was the goal to be attained. To some considerable extent that goal was realized during that century. Nevertheless, there is still some distance to travel in acceptance among Christian denominations. Some took no part in ecumenical affairs, and many campaigned aggressively against such activity, claiming it to be the work of the devil.

A defining element in the opposition to the earlier ecumenical movement was the fear of change, and of being taken over. Allied to this was a fundamentalist element that could not countenance any, as they put it, "watering down" of the faith. A major difficulty in this, of course, is deciding precisely what *faith* is being considered. This element has spilled over into interfaith matters, with its strident opposition to those whose faith stance is different.

This is visible in a number of religious stances, and has emerged in cruel and demanding ways. Truth claimed by one group, however, and considered superior to another group is in fact no truth. If we accept truth as having connection with the quality of being genuine, the question of context for and meaning of genuineness is found to be linked to particular expressions of a culture. Cultural sensitivity expresses an individual's perception of his/her life within its social and religious defining parameters. It is patently obvious that the lives of individuals are defined by their history, which includes racial features, food preferences, wealth, country of origin, and much more. It is also clear that faith persuasions also differentiate one from the other, each containing its own truth and each requiring a genuine

1.1. A Global Phenomenon

attachment. Separate faiths abound in the world. Discussion about interfaith, however, is not about encouraging all to become one. Travelling this road must ultimately deny the truths of some if a common denominator is to be found.

Stephen Prothero writes of the family of religions, and notes Ninian Smart's referral to seven dimensions of religion.[6] These he lists as ritual, narrative, experiential, institutional, ethical, doctrinal, and material:

> What makes the members of this family different . . . is how they mix and match these dimensions. Experience is central in Daoism and Buddhism. Hinduism and Judaism emphasize the narrative dimension. The ethical dimension is crucial in Confucianism. The Islamic and Yoruba traditions are to a great extent about ritual. And doctrine is particularly important to Christians.[7]

Kwok Pui-Lan, in her 2011 Madeleva Lecture, addressed the issues of *Globalization, Gender, and Peacebuilding*, with particular reference to interfaith dialogue. Raising the issue of religions claiming superiority over others, she introduces the word "polydoxy," which she says "captures the idea that Christians do not have a monopoly on God's revelation and that divinity should be understood in terms of multiplicity, open ended-ness, and relationality."[8]

Such an understanding is very difficult for many Christians, and cannot be countenanced at all by those toward the fundamentalist end of faith. Multiplicity is a claim that all religions have a place in the world. It also implies than no religious group has the right to dominate any other group. Open-endedness lays claim to the falsity in seeking to establish a religious way that has concluded it has all that is necessary for appropriate living. Strong boundaries preclude any possibility of change, or of revelation, or differences in cultural mixes. Relationality is the foundation for all of the links claimed with divinity. We live together on a small planet in a large universe. If we cannot interrelate creatively we will ultimately all die—both the people and the earth itself.

Interfaith dialogue that engages only with what people are taught and believe falls short in relationality. Labeling oneself Christian, Australian, or White is delusional if in the labeling there is some attitude of superiority and privilege. The boundaries that such an intention implies are

6. Smart, *Religious Experience of Mankind*, 15–25.
7. Prothero, *God Is Not One*, 13.
8. Pui-Lan, *Globalization, Gender, and Peacebuilding*, 70.

Part One: Interfaith—Acknowledging Differences

irrelevant in a globalized world in which all people may travel quickly, and as comfortably as they desire, into all parts of the earth. When that travel, however, has as its goal sight-seeing and pleasurable experiences, rather than meeting people, relationality will become guarded. If dialogue also becomes guarded then interfaith matters will not be clearly addressed, and unnecessary difference will continue.

When we speak of interfaith we have to be aware that faiths differ, as a result of both religious belief and of the differing cultural norms into which people have been born. To assume and then claim that there ought to be some kind of homogeneity among the world's people and their religious beliefs is to deny the fact of human diversity, of culture, and of history. Julius Lipner writes in his essay "The 'Inter' of Interfaith Spirituality":

> Too many religious people across the faiths take the title of this essay at face value, that is, they suppose that there are various different religions such as Hinduism, Christianity, Buddhism, Islam, Sikhism, and Judaism, and that bridges of different kinds—conceptual, artistic, theological, literary, etc.—can be thrown across from convenient moorings on one side or the other. This is to seriously misunderstand the 'inter' in interfaith and any attendant concept of spirituality. There is no such thing as 'Hinduism' or 'Christianity' so that one can talk simply of *the* Hindu view of life, or *the* Christian spiritual life.[9]

The matter of interfaith has, in our day, become most important in the attempt to understand and live with faith expressions that differ from our own. Driven by a realization of the global dimension of people's lives and the political upheavals that beset the world, interfaith dialogue has been seen to be an essential process for understanding. Lipner's view, however, of inadequacies in claiming discrete religious standpoints needing understanding, is important. Interfaith dialogue and its desire for understanding does appear to view faiths as separate entities and this does have a bearing on the nature of the dialogue. Christians claim a commitment to interfaith dialogue and make strong efforts to engage with others. What is frequently not taken into account, however, is that Christian interfaith dialogue mostly involves only some denominations, many others having no interest. Lipner's point needs to be taken, perhaps through a more careful reading of the meaning of the prefix *inter-*, and in any dialogue recognizing that what is being said may not be the mind of many Christians. Dialogue is complex.

9. Lipner, "'Inter' of Interfaith Spirituality," 64.

1.1. A Global Phenomenon

Spiritual life, named in terms of a particular faith stance, may be considered to be the common denominator among people. Spiritual life is interwoven into the cultural and social expression of group life. Group life, however, is not an autonomous life. Life is interwoven in a host of ways, sharing much in community. Communities within the community take from each other, all having something of value to offer. Perhaps this could become a more useful dialogue when anchored in spiritual life.

Interfaith activity is not in order to uphold the group or claim superiority; it has to do with living out one's spiritual life, being true to one's expression of that spirituality, and finding common concerns to uplift the world's people. Felix Wilfred, in his essay "Religions as Agents of Hope," reminds us that "Religious traditions are called upon to . . . activate the fountains of hope in contemporary life." This is one of the major challenges for religions in the twenty-first century. This along with other challenges "concerns the potential of religions to provide hope for a world that is drifting without a sense of direction."[10] Religious belief, and therefore those who form the diversity of religious cells, will be of little value to the world if those beliefs are directed towards the maintenance of the group, with forays into the world only in order to add to membership.

Much of the possibility for religious understanding and acceptance among groups has been derailed by political and cultural differences. Culture has a considerable influence on the playing out of interfaith understanding. Cultural and tribal differences in Africa and the Middle East, if we are to believe media reports, have caused havoc with the lives of people who want peace as they live in harmony with each other. The havoc includes murder, oppression, creation of deep fear, and genocide. Culture and religion have frequently become catalysts for all manner of behaviors, in which right is claimed through might and compulsion. Conversion or death are not good options, and indeed exacerbate the extremes of religion and culture.

A major difficulty we face in our understanding of interfaith is the linking of political and religious bodies with radical fundamentalism, and its at times blatant association with torture and death. Of particular concern in the early twenty-first century are some fundamentalist arms of Islam. One might reasonably conclude, however, that such groups are more akin to primitive tribalism than to Islam. Nevertheless, as long as this remains at the forefront of our mind—and it is bound to do so because of

10. Wilfred, "Religions as Agents of Hope," 43.

Part One: Interfaith—Acknowledging Differences

the conflicts in Iraq, Syria, and elsewhere, portrayed as they are in vivid media coverage—attempts to understand Islam will be subverted. Perhaps if we could cease using the words "Islam" and "Islamic" and instead speak of the "faith of Muslims," we would be more able to tread softly towards understanding and acceptance, and thus support all who seek changes that will allow everyone to live peaceably and safely.

It is clear, and indeed has always been so, that differences abound in the world. The differences cover virtually every aspect of our lives. Language, culture, habitat, religion—all combine to set us apart from each other. Even within language groups varieties of dialects exacerbate differences. There are in reality only two aspects in life that define any sense of commonality among people. One is that all are human, and therefore are subject to the emotions and habits that differentiate us from other animals. The other is that we live on this earth—a recurring theme in this book—and cannot get off. It therefore behooves us all to place value on all the differences, and learn to live with each other and to appreciate our common position as sojourners in the world.

1.2. Fundamentalism and Mission

FUNDAMENTALISM HAS A SOMEWHAT different face depending on which religious attachment is under consideration. The *Oxford Dictionary of English*,[1] for example, defines fundamentalism according to the faith stance. It chooses Christianity and Islam for comparison, defining fundamentalism in Christianity as the view that the Bible is divinely inspired and therefore literally true, while fundamentalism in Islam is defined as strict observance to the teachings of the Qur'an and Islamic law. Simply observing these definitions leads to the conclusion of difference. There is, however, a degree of agreement in that both definitions imply a degree of inflexibility that does not allow for additional revelation or understanding.

Interfaith can be virtually synonymous with difference, engendering for some a degree of anxiety. Difference, however, as already indicated, can be observed within all religions, not only between religious groups. Countries differ from countries, cultures differ from cultures; people differ from each other. Difference is natural and found everywhere. Religions, however, have a sameness in that they generate among their followers a sense of rightness in their belief, with a subsequent desire to share this with others and a determination that others should believe the same. For centuries now, religions, particularly Christianity and Islam, have sought, at times forcefully, to convert others and each other. This is particularly so among fundamentalist arms of religious movements. At times we abhor the fundamentalism of others, forgetting that fundamentalism is common to all. Kwok Pui-Lan supports this view with a particular comment on political life in the USA:

---

1. Stevenson, *Oxford Dictionary of English*, 709.

Part One: Interfaith—Acknowledging Differences

Religious fundamentalism of all kinds—including Christian, Islamic, Jewish and Hindu—can be seen in different parts of the world. In the United States for example, the Christian Right has a strong influence in politics and exerts great pressure to steer the country toward conservative values.[2]

Bhikhu Parekh, in his 1992 essay "The Concept of Interfaith Dialogue," comments that fundamentalism is growing all around the world, and claims it as "a response to a religious community's crisis of identity and integrity, and basically consists in reducing a complex and constantly growing tradition to a set of abstract, highly simplified and arbitrarily selected 'fundamentals' demanding total and uncritical allegiance." On the other hand, he continues, "In stark contrast to the past missionary militancy and dogmatic certitude of the great world religions, especially Christianity and Islam, there is now a refreshing attempt on their part to understand one another and to develop common areas of interest and action."[3]

In twenty years this may not be clear to all. Fundamentalism has taken on a level of activity that is dangerous to political stability throughout the world, and is of immediate threat to life and limb for millions. We need to differentiate, however, between fundamentalism and the missionary activity visible amongst world religions. Fundamentalism functions within extremes, with little or no possibilities for grey areas in its system of belief. Along with this, there is little tolerance for opposition, which is frequently met with some violence. Fundamentalists tend to be combative in their response to criticism, and there is little attention given to dialogue. Missionary activity, sometimes perceived as a claim for the minds of others, is found in the desire of a group to convert others to its beliefs. It may be aggressive in its approach, but will put reasonable arguments forward to convince others. It is recognized at times among those who door knock and seek discussion.

In both sets of activity the primary aim is to convince others of the truth in one's own faith stance as superior to the truth in the other's faith stance. Such has been the driving force among Christians, strangely enough often between Christian groups, but also in interactions with pagan and other faith groups. Larry Poston, in his study of Muslim missionary activity, recognizes similarities between the activity of the Christian churches and the current missionary outreach from Islam. Tracing the history of Islam's

---

2. Pui-Lan, *Globalization, Gender, and Peacebuilding*, 3.
3. Parekh, "Concept of Interfaith Dialogue," 158.

1.2. Fundamentalism and Mission

expansion with a particular focus on North America, he writes: "The concept of missionary activity in Islam is subsumed under the Arabic word *Da'wah*. . . . In its verbal form this word has as its basic meaning 'to call' 'to summon' 'to invite.' *Da'wah* thus becomes 'a call' or 'an invitation,' and in specialized usage, 'missionary activity.'"[4] Paul Knitter comments further:

> At the same time that Christians are admitting that centuries of missionary toil have not been able to remove the reality of religious pluralism, they witness, to their further dismay, a resurgence of missioner élan among these other religions. Hindus, Buddhists, and Muslims are claiming that their message, like that of Christianity, bears a "universal relevance."[5]

Understanding these differences is important in any provision of interfaith spiritual care. Those engaging in such care need always to be aware of difference and what this may entail. All offering spiritual care must have some awareness of the religious history of those with whom they engage, along with a sympathetic attitude to the culture that informs and supports the one receiving care. Appropriate awareness will welcome difference and recognize the creative potential available as people share their life and faith. Community cannot occur at a distance. Eyeing off the other from the citadel of our own premises will inhibit all possibility of finding the warmth of human personality in the other.

Claiming a faith citadel is also a claim to the purity of that faith, and therefore a need to defend it. The phrase "defender of the faith" is common in the Christian church, and in fact the English reigning monarch carries these words in her/his title. More ancient history, however, tells us that religious standpoints have continually come under the influence of others, such influence effecting changes in belief and understanding. Paul Knitter argues against the exclusivist truth claims of the church, seeking a new model of relationship between faiths:

> The understanding of truth–as–relational confirms . . . that, although there are real and important differences among the religions, differences that must be affirmed and confronted if dialogue is to bear fruit, these differences are, fundamentally, not contradictions but "dialogical tendencies and creative polarities." The world

---

4. Poston, *Islamic Da'wah in the West*, 3.
5. Knitter, *No Other Name?*, 4.

religions, in all their amazing differences, are more complementary than contradictory.[6]

Terry Muck, writing of the theological work of Knitter and Hick in their exploration of Christianity and other faiths, asks questions about much of current theological thinking as it reflects the core claims of Christianity. He answers:

> You cannot create a Christian theological framework that rests primarily on the wideness of God's grace and mercy, the universal presence and activity of the Holy Spirit, and the acknowledgement that all truth is God's truth, and then artificially clip out of that universality the teachings of the other religions. Theologians in the twenty-first century must do theology with and among the teachers and practitioners of Buddhist, Hindu and Muslim theologies.[7]

This, importantly, needs to become the way in which all take into account, and into their own faith living, the beliefs and practices of other religions.

John Mabry, in his 2006 book *Noticing the Divine*, makes the point that religions have been continually influenced by each other throughout the centuries. Differences in cultures have a considerable affect on religious and social life. He writes, for example, of the emergence of Zoroastrianism in Iran and traces its impact on Judaism at the time of the exile. "The contact with Zoroastrianism rendered Judaism not unrecognizable, but certainly dramatically changed from the faith the Jews had known before." This is not surprising given the length of time Jews lived in Babylon, some even finally settling there. Judaism, changed by this influence, naturally had an influence on the development of Christianity. "Without the Zoroastrian influence, Christianity as we know it would not have existed."[8]

Mabry is clear, not only in this example but throughout his book, that religious faiths interact and affect each other, and Judaism did not escape such interactions. The Hebrew scriptures themselves incorporate many of these interactions and effects. Numbers 21:8; Judges 8:33–35; and 1 Kings 11:33 are some examples of the waywardness of the Jews. Christianity declares itself to be monotheistic, but denominationalism at times casts doubts about this claim. Denominational variants could be construed at times to be presenting ideas about God that sit very loosely with the

---

6. Ibid, 220.
7. Muck, "Theology of Religions," 17.
8. Mabry, *Noticing the Divine*, 86.

1.2. Fundamentalism and Mission

established creedal position of the historic Christian faith. When we are able to recognize that in all faiths many changes have occurred through the centuries of its place in the world, we may also be prepared to acknowledge that all have been subject to outside influences.

Missionary activity that minimizes these influences, while laying claim to a particular truth as *the* truth, in effect obscures the truth. Fundamentalists' more extreme claims about the same things aggravate the spiritual life of those who are endeavouring to live out their faith. The difficulty with counterviews and extremist views is the desire to impose these as a stamp of the purity of their belief. Belief, however, can never be pure. People differ, and this is the basic fact of the matter.

This is the twenty-first century since the dating process that we have was begun. While this has its origins in Christian practice, and others have some variations in the way life is framed, there is common agreement on the centuries, years, and days that have become our guide. It is clear also that for the world to be sustained, and for people to be able to live with a degree of peace and harmony, hospitality and justice must prevail. Religious missionary activity needs to be curtailed. It is no longer appropriate for religious bodies, holding beliefs that were claimed two thousand years ago, to claim their relevance in this time. Any kind of fundamentalism also has no part in the modern world, in which all must rely on each other for life to be sustained. This may be an impossible dream, but dreaming is what we need to do. It will almost certainly be subverted by any claim of superiority, whether this be in belief or more blatantly the oppression of others.

1.3. Abraham Is Our Father

JUDAISM, CHRISTIANITY, AND ISLAM are all considered to be within the Abrahamic tradition. "Jews trace their ancestry to Abraham through his son Isaac and his grandson Jacob-Israel, Muslims trace theirs through his son Ishmael, and Christians (Gal. 3;6–7), claim descent from Abraham through faith."[1] Thus, they each trace their origins for their current understanding of connectedness to Abraham and beyond him to Abraham's God. In this venture they each lay claim to the same God, though now interpreted somewhat differently. A fundamental formula, however, lies in their heritage of having Abraham for a spiritual father, whose faith was "reckoned to him as righteousness" (Gal 3:6).

In their disputations with Jesus, religious rulers drove what they considered a final nail into the argument with their claim that they were Abraham's children. Jesus' response was: "If you were Abraham's children . . . then you would do what Abraham did" (John 8:39–40). So what is it that Abraham did? Abraham, we are told, was a wealthy man who lived in Ur in Chaldea. He was obviously a religious man for his god spoke to him and claimed his attention to a command that he pack up and leave for a country that he would be shown when he arrived. Abraham did as he was told and travelled to Haran, where he settled for a time. Eventually he continued his journey and heard promises of prosperity for himself and his people. The stories have it that Abraham maintained his faith in God, remaining true to the covenantal promise against all odds, even to offering his son Isaac for sacrifice. The inference in Jesus' words is that one cannot speak of Abraham as one's faith father if in daily living one does not maintain faith against the odds. Abraham's righteousness lay in his faithfulness. No one can therefore

---

1. Freedman, *Eerdmans Dictionary of the Bible*, 8–9.

1.3. Abraham Is Our Father

do what is wrong and destructive and still anticipate being nominated by God as righteous. A measure of spirituality therefore lies not in our heritage, which stays within the family of Christians, Muslims, and Jews, but in the degree to which we are faithful to that which creates and sustains life in order for life to be shared creatively. Recognition of our common humanity is the glue that connects us to each other. In this we are declared righteous.

The story of Abraham mirrors the movements and families of patriarchal figures who made up a considerable nomadic group, travelling from place to place throughout the Mesopotamian regions of the Middle East and down through the desert regions towards Egypt. McCarter, in his contribution to *Eerdmans Dictionary of the Bible*, writes:

> It is difficult to say whether the traditional stories about Abraham were based on the life of a historical individual and, if so, exactly when the historical Abraham might have lived. The biblical writers regarded him as a figure of the distant past, living many generations before the establishment of Israel as a political entity.[2]

Despite claims of a common spiritual ancestry, much has changed over the centuries. A major set of "overlaps and additions" that constitute a stumbling block for interfaith links can be found in the culture in which they are embedded. Irshad Manji for example, in *The Trouble with Islam*, claims that tribalism and sectarianism are endemic in Islam, having their roots in Arab culture, along with an interpretative mindset that recognizes the Qur'an as infallible.[3]

Christianity flourished throughout Europe with the blessing of kings and emperors. One does not have to travel too far into the past in England, however, or in Australia for that matter, to recognize similar aggressiveness among Christians in an era of considerable missional activity, which saw the church advancing into new worlds on the back of trade and colonization.

It is also necessary that we all constantly remind ourselves that more than half of the world's population do not lay claim to Abraham as a faith father figure. This is also a pertinent reminder for those within an Abrahamic tradition that they are not the sole beneficiaries of life with the divine. The words attributed to Jesus in Matthew's Gospel are an apt response to the claims on Abraham: "Do not presume to say to yourselves, 'We have Abraham as our ancestor'; for I tell you, God is able from these stones to

---

2. McCarter, in ibid., 9.
3. Manji, *Trouble with Islam*.

raise up children to Abraham" (Matt 3:9). There is in any claim to preferential treatment by the holy an element of superiority that is unbecoming within our global interfaith milieu. Interfaith considerations must include all expressions of religious attachment, along with a recognition of their validity and a desire to live peaceably and acceptingly within the broad spectrum of culture and faith.

Culture, as habitat, defines differences between groups along with the similarities within a group. The culture into which we are born is where we live. As such, it may be a way in which difference can be affirmed and the wonders of variety explored and enjoyed. The rituals and symbols of the culture provide body to the beliefs and actions that are part of everyday life. These may be simple or complex, but in acting them out we find our place within society, and therefore meaning for life. Belief with its ritual and culture may, however, also be a way for division, a way to differentiate and lay claim to the superiority of the insider group in all aspects that define their life.

Varieties make for complexities, and make visible the short step from here to the practice of oppression, along with a disregard for the lives of those who are outsiders. This is current practice in many countries. One may dare to assert also that in the current treatment of would-be refugees by Australia, with its underlying fear of the unknown, there is implicit oppression in the government policies in place.

The *Shorter Oxford English Dictionary* defines culture as "the training and refinement of mind, tastes, and manners; the condition of thus being trained and refined; the intellectual side of civilization."[4] In my view there is a missing element in this definition, which by its absence fails to acknowledge the differences between peoples and their commitment to the norms and customs in which their lives are set. The hierarchy implicit in the Oxford definition describes but a small segment of the meaning of culture. If we are to consider culture as a philosophy of life then ethos, values, principles, and beliefs must be acknowledged.

The tragedy in this twenty-first century is that among almost every population group values, principles, and beliefs have been damaged by an unspoken claim that "Abraham is our father." The Pharisees' claim for legitimacy on the basis of Abraham as their ancestor was in Jesus' mind of no value—"Do not presume." Claims for legitimacy surfaced strongly in

---

4. Little et al., *Shorter Oxford English Dictionary*, 471.

1.3. Abraham Is Our Father

the Australian Government's Royal Commission into sexual abuse.[5] One religious group under examination decided over many years not to report abuse claims to police, nor do much else than counsel offenders. Victims were given little help. Under a general umbrella of presumption, we destroy ourselves and others in our indulgences with drugs. With presumptions of a sound relationship with God, we terrorize and destroy with utter disregard for others. Blind adherence, however, to inheritance claims that have their origins in myth is a catalyst for tragedy. What was required of the Pharisees, and what is required of us whether or not we trace our religious inheritance to Abraham, is a commitment to understanding and embracing difference in this one global world in which we live. If this does not happen, the future could be bleak.

Metamorphosis is a synonym for difference, and there are a number of definitions attached to it, of which two are valuable for our purposes. One of these is: "A complete change of character, appearance etc." The other: "A rapid transformation of a larvae into an adult."[6] My question is whether there is another way of considering interfaith conversation and understanding through this process of metamorphosis. If we, as Buber suggests, *are a dialogue*,[7] it follows that if the dialogue is sincere and honest, with regard and respect for the other, something of a metamorphosis might be anticipated. The definitions listed above are of particular interest in the dialogic process.

One of those definitions speaks of the "transformation of a larvae into an adult." The larvae as the primary primitive form of the animal may be likened to the beginnings of a dialogue in which people of differing faiths approach each other hesitantly and with some fear of its direction. Such an initial approach will be inhibited by presuppositions, biases, and feelings of religious superiority, or maybe insecurity. Adulthood in dialogue is reached when those who approach each other recognize in each other a common humanity in which, despite differences in beliefs, needs, wants, and desires, relationality can be discerned. Amongst all people needs for shelter, food, clean water, companionship, order, justice, freedom, love, and more can be found. The adult, recognizing these things in him/herself, along with recognition of these matters in others, has entered a time of metamorphosis.

---

5. It met in 2013–2015 in response to innumerable claims of sexual abuse against churches and other groups who cared for children.

6 Makins, *Collins Concise Dictionary*, 836.

7. Buber, *Between Man and Man*, 17–22.

Part One: Interfaith—Acknowledging Differences

Metamorphosis requires a time of quiet withdrawal in which to ponder the strengths and weaknesses of our own faith standpoint. This must include both the established doctrinal claims and our own response. A metamorphosis results in a considerable change, from a caterpillar that can only crawl into a butterfly that can take off and fly into a new realm. This is an obvious character shift in the insect world, and may for our life be an appropriate analogy in which it can be further recognized from the second definition above as a considerable change of character and appearance in the movement from wary mistrust to trust and openness. The journey thus far can be considered a step on the way to friendship and a commitment to acknowledge differences as expressions of one's life. Furthermore, we will begin to understand that there should not be an expectation that all should believe the same or live identical lives.

Claims for legitimacy based on religious data first promulgated thousands of years ago are a confession of our failure to recognize that events and happenings come and go, and can hold us for only a brief time if we are to grow and mature. When these claims for legitimacy continue to be based on events long gone, we begin to be seen as little children playing a game and wanting everyone to play the same game.

It is clear, however, that not even those who may be broadly recognized as belonging in the same group play the same game. As I have said elsewhere, my background is Christian, and from that background I can make the bold claim that within Christianity there are considerable differences. Christians may all make claims of commonality in Abraham, but in their religious life commonality is variable. From the two ends of a Christian continuum we can be sure there is little in common to link the two ends together. I imagine that the same may be said for many religious standpoints.

1.4. Interfaith—Finding God

If interfaith conversations are taken with some hope that participants will find God, the primary purpose of the conversation will be lost. One difficulty experienced by Christians lies in the claim to know the name of God as Jesus Christ. What Moses (Exod 3:13) couldn't find, Christians have. The difficulty lies in giving the impression that there is an intimate connection that others don't have. Being an insider, as it were, implies that others are outsiders. When others consider this a presumptuous claim, dialogue becomes most difficult. It is generally most difficult for Christians to think that any response to their message may be an indignant one. Any sense of the other's belief as somehow being inferior implies, if not stated outright, that the other is wrong and needs to change. This has been the church's message for centuries, but it can no longer be held as containing necessary truth. We can no longer as Christians claim to know the true God, and define *him* in terms of Jesus.

Conversations occur for a variety of reasons between people and groups. Some are undertaken as information sharing, some to reach a decision for action, and some to seek consensus on particular issues. Interfaith conversation, perhaps more focused as dialogue, is in the first instance seeking understanding. For this to happen beliefs and attitudes that we hold dear need to be placed to one side. They are not discarded, but placing them to one side allows a more uncluttered pathway towards understanding. With understanding comes hope of a more relational and peaceful future. An important question for all religious groups, and their individual members, has to do with the effect of religious difference. Stephan Prothero, in his book *God Is Not One*, highlights difference and offers the following insight:

Part One: Interfaith—Acknowledging Differences

feelings of fear and awe. Of the religious of social experience Shinn says, "in the acquisition of a social religious reality, cultural norms and sanctions are often included as a part of the institutional and familial socialization processes. Such an inclusion is especially likely when the socially accepted everyday reality is construed to be consistent with religious reality."[4]

History demonstrates that as individual experiences of the divine are shared, there comes a time when the sharing begins to be codified, set down as a group viewing, and becoming organized with a declared understanding of the divine. Having taken over from individuals, the organization subsumes them into the whole. Thus all the great religious movements were born and began to grow. With the growth comes additions and accretions, the practice of the body's faith life. In Australia, the national social institution we call "government" retains an earlier supposition of government and nation as Christian in the regular recital of the Lord's Prayer and other formal prayers as it begins its deliberations. Denominations of the Christian church must also be recognized through legislation and regulation before becoming church. Rituals and symbols differ, but are acceptable in both social and religious life.

We can also assert that within Christianity denominationalism indicates differences in faith understanding. Such differences are clearly visible within the church. These differences have at times taken on the nature of interfaith understandings rather than differences of opinion within the same blanket religious stance. It is common, for example, to hear among Christians references to such as the "Catholic faith," "Anglican faith," "Baptist faith," and so on. Islam, Buddhism, Hinduism, and others also contain denominations in which we will find variations in the articulation of religious views and understandings. Edward Conze, for example, says of Buddhism:

> The bulk of authoritative Buddhist writings is truly enormous, and covers tens and hundreds of thousands of pages. The Pali Canon, which is restricted to one single sect, fills 45 huge volumes in the complete Siamese edition, exclusive of commentaries. The Chinese and Tibetan Canons, on the other hand, include all of those schools which left their mark on China or Tibet.[5]

"Different schools", says Conze, "wrote down different things."[6] Personally and socially, the engendering of hope is of critical importance.

4. Ibid, 39.
5. Conze, *Buddhist Scriptures*, 11.
6. Ibid., 12.

1.4. Interfaith—Finding God

Strongly held opinions, frequently visible in denominational claims across the range of all faith stances, do not allow for openness in dialogue, nor bode well for authentic listening to and respect for another. Lacking these suggests they also lack some ability to engender hope.

So what do I mean when I say in the heading of this chapter "finding God"? God is not an object to be "found." We cannot search for God as we might a cricket ball. The cultural experience in any search for God will result in an encultured God, one who fits the desires and hopes of the people. If there was only one cultural expression in the world, it might work. The reality, as we are well aware, is vastly different. Arguments about the validity of God will always carry the culture's particular understanding about life. Conversation about human life may be a more open way to develop our understanding of the nature of the divine. Finding God is more akin to becoming aware of sacred presence—a sense of otherness or holiness—in the conversation. Difficulties remain as faiths endeavor to describe their links to their god/s and at times seek to justify the explanations.

What we all seem to forget at times is that among all cultural, language, and ethnic groups there are many ways to conceive of the holy in our lives. Understanding the nature of the divine in daily life is what provides meaning for living, but meaning also is caught up in the aspects of life that makes a group what it is. The divine, though appearing in different forms, seems universally to be located somewhere away from the believer. A more helpful understanding is to take a more holistic view that may recognize the holy in the qualities that enhance our daily living.

As people gather together we will discover in the group those who love to talk and those who prefer to listen. Physical shape and emotional ability vary greatly. Cultural background has a considerable effect. All cultures contain mini-cultures, such as a family, a particular neighborhood, a faith group, and more. In each and every one of these differences the dialogue that presents itself must be accommodated if together the participants are to find common ground. Recognizing that the primary common ground is our humanity enables us to find our own responses to this commonality, and a recognition of our own place in this. If we are the dialogue, then words spoken will illuminate who we are relationally to the other. In the unfolding of the relationship, as we attend to each other's words and feelings, awareness creeps in, and we may recognize something of the divine.

1.5. Hospitality in Dialogue among Difference

THE ENGENDERING OF HOPE is a most important element in interfaith dialogue. All religious formulations, it would appear, are much better at defending their faith and more free at explaining nuances of meaning than they are at offering hospitality for the world's people. No doubt, it is important in all faith persuasions that adherents understand the basic tenets of their faith. It is also important for the peace of a world in which justice is clearly served that people find hope for their lives in the symbols and rituals so carefully explained. Having hope as a companion allows for attitudes to change and others to be acceptable.

Attitudes, however, can have a telling effect on hospitality. Feelings of superiority over other tribes, races, and caste systems all work against hospitality. Even in Australia right now we have a de facto caste system. It is ethnic—Aborigines on the lowest rung—and it is religious—Christianity on the top rung. The Queensland Uniting Church Synod Interfaith Relations Committee seeks ongoing dialogue with other faiths. In such dialogue doors towards hospitality may be opened and others invited in. The problem is that at times the church is its own worst enemy. One of the members of that committee preached a sermon during a worship service. Part of the sermon considered the story of the Samaritan woman and the discussion with Jesus about worship:

> Jesus does not invalidate her worship but proclaims her worship as valid though she does not know the truth of who she is worshipping. . . . How does God treat this worship? We do not have the answers, and in relationship with other faiths we will never know how God relates to their worship. However we DO know

1.5. Hospitality in Dialogue among Difference

> something, if Jesus does not invalidate her worship then neither should we. This, however, does not mean that we need accept that it is *true* worship (. . .) we don't back away from our truth claim; all worship is not equal, salvation comes from Jesus, no one else.[1]

The claim—all worship is not equal—is a value judgement that has no basis in any context. Both interfaith relations and hospitality fail at this point. Worship is a peoples' response to what they consider an experience of the sacred in their lives. Denying this as legitimate is a denial of the faith life of people. Claiming it as inferior to one's own expression of worship fails to take account of the words and actions of Jesus as the claimed founder of the Christian faith. A claim of superiority such as this leaves us mired in church dogma, and dogma itself is at times very sticky. Despite affirming certain things about the other, distance continues when we deny the validity of another's place vis-a-vis the sacred. We can affirm each other as human beings, but fail in our understanding of *being*. This appears as a problem in dialogue, is common to all religious forms, and expresses a desire for recognition of the truth of one's own faith stance. Kearney and Taylor make the point that:

> Interreligious hospitality is a primary task of our time. We say task because, like, most other universally desirable virtues, we are never done with hospitality. There are always more guests to be hosted, ever new strangers to be welcomed as they arrive at the door bearing gifts or challenges, asking for bread or refuge, questioning, calling, demanding, thanking. And there are many different kinds of strangers, not only those aliens and others who come from afar, but also those strangers who come from within ourselves.[2]

Guests and strangers require dialogue, if understanding is to occur. Dialogue facilitates hospitality.

Dialogues, however, deal with words and frequently become bogged down in meanings of the words rather than the matter which they seek to portray. The Christian church, itself divided for centuries, has undertaken many dialogues between denominations, but despite some headway, and the commitment of participants, it does not appear to be much closer to resolving the difficulties. Hans Kung, arguing the importance of dialogue, makes the point that:

---

1. From a Sermon, preached in a Christian woship service.
2. Kearney et al, *Hosting the Stranger*, 1.

Part One: Interfaith—Acknowledging Differences

> The boundary between true and false today, even as Christians see it, no longer runs simply *between* Christianity and other religions, but at least in part *within* each of the religions. The principle here is that nothing of value in the other religions is to be denied, but neither is anything of no value to be uncritically accepted. On this score a consensus should be possible among representatives of the various religions. We need a dialogue of give and take, into which the deepest intentions of the religions must be introduced.[3]

Openness and frankness, as sources of hospitality, are not always visible even between denominations, which suggests that if denominational solutions are so difficult within one faith's religious framework how much greater is the difficulty crossing faith boundaries—particularly so when the vehicle used is words. There is clearly a need for a different vehicle, driven differently. We need, therefore, to first recognize that despite differences in religious understanding and cultural behavior, and despite the complexities in interfaith dialogue, there are human attributes that are common to all, one of which could be said to be awareness of transcendence in some form. This is strongly linked to the way in which people seek meaning, and it is within this search that possibilities for interfaith spiritual care emerge. Dialogue is normally considered in the context of conversation, exchange of opinions, and its variation within religious and faith understandings. This, it appears, is simply not adequate, and is certainly not conducive to hospitality.

Kenneth Kramer's paper published in the *Journal of Ecumenical Studies* is a commentary on interfaith dialogue. He refers to both Abraham Heschel and Martin Buber, whose insights are important critiques of current interfaith conversation. Heschel, Kramer writes, claims four components as primary in interfaith conversations:

> First, the most important *prerequisite* is faith, described as inwardness. . . . Second, the most significant *basis* for meeting people of other faiths is to meet as human beings who have much in common. . . . Third, the *process* of interfaith dialogue is the mutual enrichment and enhancement of respect and appreciation. . . . Fourth, undergirding and supporting the first three components of interfaith dialogue is the maintenance of a faith shaping, purpose expanding sense of *possibility*.[4]

---

3. Kung, *Christianity and the World Religions*, xviii.
4. Kramer, "Jesus, as a Jew," 610–11.

1.5. Hospitality in Dialogue among Difference

Kramer continues, with reference to Martin Buber,[5] that Buber claims "we are a dialogue." Buber himself writes:

> A dialogical relation will show itself also in genuine conversation, but it is not composed of this. Not only is the shared silence of two such persons a dialogue, but also their dialogical life continues, even when they are separated in space, as the continual potential presence of the one to the other, as an unexpressed intercourse. On the other hand, all conversation derives its genuineness only from the element of inclusion even if this appears only abstractedly as an "acknowledgement" of the actual being of the partner in the conversation; but this acknowledgement can be real and effective only when it springs from an experience of inclusion, of the other side.[6]

Dialogue requires mutuality and the commitment of both elements of the dialogue to engage, despite the complexities of mixed faiths. Complexities inherent in the multiplicity of faith standpoints throughout the world should be acknowledged, but not minimized.

Having said all that, it must also be said that dialogues do continue, and open possibilities for greater understanding. As interfaith conversations and meetings continue, there is a developing desire to acknowledge the validity of the other religion, and an acknowledgement that any one religious standpoint may not contain the whole truth. In a commentary on Hindu-Christian dialogue, Klostermaier concludes:

> By meeting the other, each side is reminded of its own roots and original beliefs, over against which later events and developments leading to fissions and divisions may appear relatively unimportant. Such dialogue perhaps will lead to a more essential and more relevant Christianity and Hinduism.[7]

Similar comments may be made of other dialogues between, for example, Buddhists and Christians. These official dialogues provide a measure of congruity without seeking to embed one within the other. An even more helpful dialogue is between individuals who share their faith from within their own faith, and begin to truly understand the other as a person of faith.

Such complexities raise enormous problems. Paul Knitter writes, for example, of the Indian religious experience as one of successive waves of

---

5. Ibid, 612.
6. Buber, *Between Man and Man*, 125.
7. Klostermaier, "Hindu-Christian Dialogue," 521.

Part One: Interfaith—Acknowledging Differences

invasion and the imposition of religion. "The historical track record of religion in India . . . is that of an agent of animosity rather than of amity." He says a little later, "Against background of both history and daily newspapers, religion in India appears to be much more of an intercommunal weapon than an intercommunal bond."[8] This pattern we can see repeated again and again in the history of colonial and religious expansionism.

Such complexities of belief among faith groups are clearly outlined by Fitzgerald and Borelli in their book *Interfaith Dialogue: A Catholic View*:

> If you want to bring greeting to the Muslims for *'Id al-Fitr*, the breaking of the fast after Ramadam, or *'Id al-Adha*, the Feast of the Sacrifice held in concomitance with the *Hajj*, the Pilgrimage to Mecca, then you have to know when the feast will take place in any particular year. The same goes for *Vesakh* of the Buddhists, or *Diwali* of the Hindus. And what festival are the Sikhs celebrating. It is easy to lump all the Muslims into one, and not to realize that they belong to very different traditions. It would be useful to have an inkling about what they hold in common, and how they differ. Similarly with the Buddhists. That monastery in the suburbs of the town; to which group does it belong? Is the Dalai Lama really a sort of Buddhist pope? One could go on and on with such questions. And the more one learns, the more one realizes how little one knows.[9]

They make a further point that "Dialogue will be impossible, or at least extremely difficult, where minds are closed. If there is a conviction that only I have the truth, and that the other person is completely in error, then there can be no true meeting of minds. Such a closed mentality will have to be overcome."[10] This is critical in the practice of hospitality.

The point is made by the authors of *Getting to the Heart of Interfaith* that "Interfaith . . . points towards activities or relationships between people of different beliefs or faith identities."[11] Differences in understandings and expressions of faith in interfaith interactions are core elements in any difficulty experienced in interfaith engagements. What is needed, therefore, is at least an understanding of the way in which others think of faith. Mackenzie et al. explain it as follows:

---

8. Knitter, *One Earth, Many Religions*, 160.
9. Fitzgerald and Borelli, *Interfaith Dialogue*, 65.
10. Ibid., 90.
11. Mackenzie et al., *Getting to the Heart of Interfaith*, 6

1.5. Hospitality in Dialogue among Difference

> When Pastor Don uses the word faith he is talking about a way of understanding experience that is grounded in a trust in God, a trust that gives us what we need to cooperate with God's purposes, to do God's will. . . . Christians see life through the eyes of faith. . . . When Rabbi Ted uses the Hebrew word *emunah*, which is often translated as "faith," it signifies firmness and is related more to action than to belief. This firmness indicates a kind of faithfulness in the sense of reliability and can be translated as "it is so"-ness. When Sheikh Jamal uses the word faith he is referring to the Qur'an's teaching which specifies that a Muslim must build faith in God, angels, prophets, holy books, and the Day of Judgement. In these five beliefs the devotee must move from *borrowed certainty* to what the Holy Book calls *inner certainty*.[12]

Trust in God; *It is so*; *inner certainty*: are these, we might ask, the core statements embedded in the above? If so, can they be said to be saying essentially the same thing? If this is so, is the difficulty in the interfaith journey more about what might be considered peripheral matters? Questions such as these need answering if clarity is to be realized. A problem with making any such assumption is that we can be accused of reductionism and this is of course a legitimate criticism. It is not my intention, however, to reduce faith to such a few words. Rather, it is a desire to focus on something that might be regarded as a core proposition on which understanding may be built.

Understanding occurs as a result of being hospitable, but it also grows out of the practice of hospitality. Hospitality is practiced to some degree in all religions. In some faiths it is integral to the faith of followers and in some instances is also a recognized cultural norm. Klostermaier, in his survey of Hinduism, notes of hospitality among Hindus and the Indian subcontinent that "India still has a tradition of hospitality that has no parallel in the contemporary West. Wealthy pious Hindus of the past and the present have established numerous guest houses in places of pilgrimage; these . . . offer usually free shelter and quite frequently free food to travelers and pilgrims, irrespective of their creed or colour."[13]

Hospitality comes naturally for some, even among difference. Hospitality, of course, is not only about inviting someone to dinner. Hospitality is a framework for living in which we can affirm all people for the sake of humanity, and perhaps also in the name of that which is holy for us.

---

12. Ibid., 6–7.
13. Klostermaier, "Hindu-Christian Dialogue," 164.

Part One: Interfaith—Acknowledging Differences

Hospitality needs to become a natural way for interaction with others. This doesn't mean that we go out of our way to be nice to everyone. That is really a dream. Being hospitable can be a way of life that values others' way of life and is supportive of things that seek the good of others. In our world of difference, acknowledging the value of difference can itself be a hospitable act.

1.6. Habitat

HABITAT IS DEFINED IN the *Oxford Dictionary of English* as "a natural home."[1] Habitat speaks to place, relationship, familiarity, community, sharing, peace, justice, and being. Attachment to habitat allows residents to share food and drink, to gather in a common space for games and talk and conviviality. It accommodates everybody from frail elderly to babes in arms, and all in between. It provides identity in the social and religious ambiance in which all have a place. The people may be poor but poverty is shared in the warmth of relationship. Informal rules provide a structure within which people can feel safe. Habitat is the place where people are normally found. What are some of these places? In the first place, we have to name the earth. We are all citizens of the earth. Within the whole of the universe, circulating in the vastness of space, earth is our home. We describe the earth as an inhabited planet. Because through millennia people have dispersed all over the land, habitats vary from person to person and group to group. Language groups, racial groups, and tribal groups have naturally settled together and come to know the place in which they have settled as their own.

This has not always been a happy or peaceful process. Because of our differences, and because of differences in land quality, jealousy and envy has arisen from time to time and spilled over into claims on land. In this period of the twenty-first century such disputes are continuing with tragic results for the habitats of people and disastrous results for their life. These habitats are the local areas where people have settled, built houses for shelter, and raised families. These are places in which people work at a variety of tasks to earn their keep. Carrie Doehring, in her paper "Teaching an

1. Stevenson, *Oxford Dictionary of English*, 786.

Intercultural Approach to Spiritual Care," speaks of each person's religious world as a habitat.[2] Religious habitat is a place in which people can draw near to and feel comfortable with whoever they consider to be divine. Thus we have in the world many religious habitats. One of the difficulties associated with this is that residents of some habitats consider their place to be of more value than the others, and that those others would be better placed if they changed habitats. Aggressive missionary activity over the centuries has demonstrated this.

Thinking about religious life leads me to consider that any attempt to seek conversions from one faith to another faith is an uprooting of another's abode in which they find comfort and meaning. Habitats can be reshaped by natural disaster to the extent that whole neighborhoods may relocate to a different place. The lives of residents may face considerable disruption. Such relocation, however, may include decisions by the residents so that, even though disruptive, repositioning is manageable. Physical relocation may also have an impact on religious behavior, depending on the magnitude of the move. Those who already have a strong religious connection will find ways to re-establish that. Doehring makes this plain:

> While the term religious world or home helps us to visualize the uniqueness of each person's religious faith and spirituality, it doesn't help us appreciate how religious worlds are continually constructed and reconstructed within relational matrices and not within a person's mind. From a relational perspective one's religious world or home involves a layering of multiple religious and spiritual symbols, beliefs and schema, all generated out of one's relational matrices, past and present.[3]

Such a layering may be found in the three major religious faith groups of Judaism, Christianity, and Islam. The very nature of Christianity is to shift its shape constantly as people desire change for their life, and the processes they engage in for meaning making in their lives. Habitat has a number of levels of influence, and at each level of understanding difficulties are generated by people who differ. The differences are in our heritage, and we are all attached to families and groups and nations in which we claim identity. Many of the differences are natural and should give no offence to anyone. Habitat extends far more widely than attachment to families and groups, even nations. Carolyn King's statement that "The first and

2. Doehring, "Teaching an Intercultural Approach," 2.6.
3. Ibid., 2.6.

1.6. Habitat

basic requirement for the health of the whole inhabited earth, is that it be habitable"[4] is one we should be concerned about as we consider the implications of our impact on the world we live in.

Secure habitat is a precious commodity, the disruption of which has a profound impact on inhabitants. When people have lived in a place for generations—when they have worked and tilled the land, when they have sat around a fire in warm companionship, when they have protected and sustained each other—their sense of presence can be palpable. Losing one's home to the ravages of an earthquake or mud slide can be a gateway to despair. The effects of that despair on people's lives can be seen at times in the faces of those who have lost all.

Communities develop in many ways. They don't have to be blood relations, but common language, habits, culture, and locality all combine to establish a sense of belonging. I think also that community pre-supposes a spirit presence. This may have little to do with religion or gods but it provides a degree of commonality and adherence.

When conflict erupts as a result of interfaith or intrafaith clashes, damage is inflicted not only on people but also on the earth itself. Homes, hospitals, workplaces, orchards, and gardens are pummeled by indiscriminate use of shells and bombs and rockets. Habitat is frequently grievously damaged, and the residue is often bitterness. A pulverized earth suffers greatly, along with those who struggle to live, and peace and justice are nowhere visible. As this is being written, in many parts of the world, whatever the roots of conflict might be, news bulletins show enormous destruction of habitat, with people left bereft of all their possessions, mourning the loss of loved ones, and brooding over a sense of total hopelessness. The violent shattering of habitat, as is occurring at this time in countries such as Syria and Iraq, will influence the lives of inhabitants for generations.

Television images remind us that for so many habitat has become a temporary dwelling with remote possibilities of permanency among people whose lives have been fragmented beyond repair. It is also true, however, that many people choose a migratory life. This has been the norm among some groups of travelers. Whether in the United Kingdom or in Siberia, traditional travelers find community in their lifestyle attachments. Habitat is guaranteed by the group's cohesion.

In an earlier chapter we recognized that people can be said to bear an image of the sacred. Attacks on habitat in which people are destroyed

---

4. King, *Habitat of Grace*, 29.

could be seen as the destruction of an intangible part of life that is linked to spirit. Could this leave the spirit homeless? It would seem, listening to people whose homes have been destroyed, that some sense a spiritual loss. One could suggest that a wandering spirit exacerbates any sense of loss. A synonym for habitat is "haunt," a place of meeting amongst other things. Is it possible, I wonder, that the spirits attached to habitats may return to haunt that place and wreak vengeance on the destroyers? Fantasy perhaps, but if the sense of spirit presence was real for the people whose homes were destroyed, could it not be possible that the spirits continue to occupy the space?

King, in her book *Habitat of Grace*, quotes Moltmann, who says: "The long established interest of the churches in peace and justice for humans was not enough by itself; there can be no peace and justice for us, unless we also protect the natural world."[5] Protection of the habitat must include a recognition of the earth as alive. When land is destroyed, when pollution is rife, when the earth overheats, disaster looms. When people fight each other, frequently with great ferocity, habitat diminishes and people become fearful and lost. Fighting between groups, frequently in the name of religion and claims of the superiority and rightness of their beliefs, denies the spirit and ignores the one we name as sacred, or worse, considers the spirit of no account.

Charles Birch, in the introduction to his book *On Purpose*, claims that at the time of writing (and I suggest it is still true today):

> There is widespread conflict between our conception of ourselves and our conception of the world. We see ourselves as beings that are conscious, that are rational, have free will and are purposive. But we see the world as consisting of mindless, meaningless, totally determined physical bits and pieces that are non–purposive. A society that lives with this dichotomy is operating out of a profound error that is destroying much that is worthwhile both in ourselves and in the world.[6]

Any notion that people are rational and purposive beings is a complete misconception. The terrors from wars and diseases that stalk across much of the world, our addictions to excesses in alcohol and drug consumption, our grasping for wealth, and our failures in embracing responsibility for our excesses clearly express an irrationality in life. Conscious intention

---

5. Ibid., 30.
6. Birch, *On Purpose*, ix.

1.6. Habitat

appears at times to be focused only on personal gain. The earth, however, is not something we designed for ourselves. It is not our spaceship carrying us from one realm to another. The earth is ours by grace. It is a gift from which we have torn the wrapping and plundered for our profit instead of carefully and lovingly entering into a mutual relationship that is life-giving.

People are not always good at receiving gifts. Frequently there is an underlying question about the motive in gift giving: "What does he/she want from me?" It is almost as if suspicion is second nature to all of us. So few are able to simply respond, "Thank you." The all-important response, however, asks, "What am I going to do with this gift?" The earth has been gifted to us along with the gift of life. We must, therefore, if we are to look after the twin gifts of life and habitat, treasure and share them, and preserve them for those following.

PART TWO

Spiritual Care—Bridging the Differences

IN THE PRACTICALITIES OF life, boundaries and borders have at times taken on considerable significance. Barriers have been erected at times and continue to be erected to keep some out and others in. Historically, natural barriers like rivers and deep valleys kept people apart and perhaps preserved a degree of peace. Once the possibility for crossing was realized and bridges began, boundaries were crossed and barriers removed. In our day rivers are crossed interminably every day. Boundaries have largely ceased to be rigid, and people can move more freely, even from country to country and culture to culture.

It is stating the obvious when acknowledging the considerable diversity in culture, nationhood, and religious affiliation among the world's people. It is also abundantly clear that there are many racial attributes that distinguish people from each other. Common to all people, however, is the presence of suffering. Natural disasters frequently have the effect of bridging difference. Disasters that occur through the exercise of such as political power and religious extremism exacerbate the difference. Individuals at times suffer discrimination and are made to feel their difference when seeking asylum from persecution and travail. Difficulties with language, and with being an element of a minority group, enlarge difference rather than diminish it. Spiritual care, as a way of exploring hopes and fears among this diversity and difference, along with the additional complexities associated with the beliefs of differing faith communities, is a demanding and uncertain journey. It must, however, be undertaken when requested.

Part Two: Spiritual Care—Bridging the Differences

Spiritual care as a mutual search for meaning must take account of human *being*. Spiritual care does not locate the one being cared for within a specific religious framework. Rather, it locates the one receiving care within a human framework, as a fundamentally spiritual being. Spiritual care lays claim to the wholeness of persons, a wholeness that includes all that is seen and unseen. It can become the bridge that enables people to cross difficult boundaries. The search for meaning may find a place for this or that individual within a particular faith stance, but that is not the primary aim. If in the process a specific faith stance that is valued by the one receiving care emerges, it should be applauded as a goal discovered. Discovery is perhaps always the goal in the search for meaning, even if only a goal on the way.

Spiritual care may be recognized as containing a number of elements that can be named as descriptors of its component parts, each of which may be considered a bridge over boundaries. These are:

2.1 Dancing God

2.2 Tell Them *I Am*

2.3 On *Being*, and Meeting the Sacred

2.4 Listening

2.5 Meditation

2.6 Presence

These are examined separately to detect the values that we can ascribe to spiritual care as a most appropriate way to engage pastorally with others, no matter what the nature of their belief may be.

2.1. Dancing God

HEALTH CARE IS A focused business needing to tackle a considerable variety of issues. The culture and religious attitudes of those seeking care is therefore irrelevant to the matter of health care even though some cultural and religious norms may have to be overcome for the care to be applied. The provision of pastoral care also has to take notice of these cultural and religious norms, but in a different way.

Carey and Daveron conducted a study in Australia in which they examined Australian health care systems and the need for changes in pastoral activity. Introducing their report on "Interfaith Pastoral Care and the Role of the Health Care Chaplain," appearing in the *Scottish Journal of Healthcare Chaplaincy*, they state:

> Over the last thirty years the face of health care within all Australian capital cities has changed substantially, particularly in meeting the various needs of people from other cultures who have migrated from distant shores as a result of poverty, persecution and war. Ministering to an increasing number of people who are from different cultural backgrounds and from non-Christian religions has the potential to present various challenges to Christian chaplains working within clinical contexts.[1]

The challenges that face chaplains have to do not only with the significance of multiple faith stances, but also with a lack of focus among chaplains, and within pastoral care departments. Historically pastoral care consisted, in the main, of representatives of individual churches visiting their congregation members and seeking to maintain them in a Christian framework. This is still possible and in many ways an adequate approach to

---

1. Carey and Daveron, "Interfaith Pastoral Care," 21.

those who are linked to their church. It becomes inadequate when chaplains continue to carry their faith stance into interactions with people who have a completely different faith stance but still appreciate a caring visit. We have not yet grasped the significance of difference, nor the fact that the Christian message is not required by those whose lives are immersed in a different belief framework. This is perhaps the most important change required in chaplaincy outlook. Within a culture that has been largely Christian, and in which the claims of Christianity have been assumed in the church to be its primary motivation, any attempt to move away from this generates considerable anxiety. Stephen Prothero raises important points for all who have difficulty moving from their customary faith stance.

> One of the most common misconceptions about the world's religions is that they plumb the same depths, ask the same questions. They do not. Only religions that see God as all good ask how a good God can allow millions to die in Tsunamis. Only religions that believe in souls ask whether your soul exists before you are born and what happens to it after you die. And only religions that think we have one soul ask after "the soul" in the singular. Every religion however, asks after the human condition. Here we are in these bodies. What now? What next? What are we to become?[2]

These are indeed important questions for the people of the earth, not just the church. In all of the earth's countries there are some who are immensely rich and many who are immensely poor. There are those who take on the guise of religion, and act as primitive tribalists performing acts of terror as they claim attachment to their God. Throughout the world there is poverty, injustice, and abuse. The diversity of human life is enormous. How then is it possible to discover meaning? The answer is that if the question is applied to the whole it is not possible to discover meaning.

Meaning starts small, and spiritual care can have a hand in this. Meaning must encompass something of the sacred, but this requires a voyage of discovery. I think in some way religions are a voyage of discovery. Each religion, in which teachings are established, rituals practiced, and people called to participate, is a voyage of discovery. For centuries, throughout the world, religious dreams have materialized and pronouncements been made that affect people's lives. Their voyage continues. This voyage is hindered when all religions are named as if they were a homogenous entity. The reality is that homogeneity cannot be attributed to any. The complexities

---

2. Prothero, *God Is Not One*, 24.

2.1. Dancing God

become clear even in the consideration of just one of the many. The term "Christianity," for example, is a title applied to all who claim a particular relationship with their God. The reality is that Christianity is a fragmented religion with a large number of denominational groupings, many of which present considerable differences in the expression of their belief. Denominationalism has been plagued by suspicion and arguments for the truth of particular standpoints. At times the divisions have been bitter. Today some of this still remains.

The heritage of religions is not a happy one. Rather, the world has inherited much trouble and strife. It is strange that religions claiming eternal life in a paradisical place with joy, contentment, and affinity with the holy should repeatedly fight and argue with each other over claims of possession of greater truth, and therefore the right or only pathway worth travelling. Even stranger is our recognition that although we are individuals we all, in one way or another, participate in this strife. How then might we find an adequate way for spiritual care?

True spiritual care seeks, in company with others, pathways to meaningful living. In a foreword to *Making Health Care Whole* (2010), Rachel Remen recounts a story that makes evident the spiritual dimension of life and the interfaith component that must always be considered. She writes of a piece of sacred art projected onto a screen. The one that engraved itself on her memory was:

> A small bronze of a dancing Shiva, the god of creation, from a museum in Europe. I remember being struck by the beauty and joy of the little figure, dancing with abandon in a ring of bronze flame, one foot lifted high in the air and the other resting on the back of a little man, crouched in the dust, completely absorbed in something he was holding between his hands.

"That little man," she writes, "is someone who is so caught up in the study of the material world that he does not know that the living god is dancing on his back."[3]

Christians offering spiritual care need to remember that at times the Christian desire for the transformation of the world, with the language of salvation, is rather more like the little man than the dancing God. Christianity, expressed publicly in the church, has more often than not followed the activity of the little man. There is a seriousness about Christianity with

---

3. Remen, in Puchalski and Ferrell, *Making Health Care Whole*, xiii.

its focus on sin, salvation, and doing. But if salvation is only preparation for another life, what about this life now?

I wonder at times what might occur if we were to consider the life of Jesus as a creative action in which he sought to open pathways to new behaviors. His teaching, as it appears in the Gospels, takes hold of familiar things and then considers other options for action that are life-giving. The healings as portrayed in the Gospels provide new opportunities. "The blind see, the lame walk." The bedridden "take up their beds." Jesus' short public life opened vistas in which people might dance and scatter light.

The creation stories can be recognized as embracing the dancing God image. As the world takes shape through light and dark, earth and sea, plants and animals, overseen, as it were, by glittering stars, God reflects on each *day* and acknowledges it all as good. The complex interactions and relationships are more indicative of the dancing God than of a methodical, getting-it-all-right God. Human life is never methodical; an infinite variety is more akin to the ring of bronze flame flowing from the dancing figure.

Spiritual care, we might argue, is an assisted search for meaning within a given understanding of the sacred. This can be a prolonged and serious search. Is it possible, therefore, for spiritual care to become an invitation to dance? I think yes! One function of spiritual care is helping to unravel difficulties. One patient with whom I spent some time over a period of months told the following story:

> I imagined myself struggling with fishing line that was tangled round my hands and feet. My niece and two children were visiting me and I asked her and the children to help me get it off. She tried to explain that there was no fishing line on me. Our minister came at this stage and my niece explained what was happening. He held me and comforted me and quietly went through the motions of untying the line from my hand and feet, talking to me all the time and explaining what he was doing. He then took the imaginary line out and threw it away. I felt at ease then and free of being tied down.[4]

When one is beset by fears it is like being entangled in a mire of unfocused happenings and relationships. The more the entanglement, the less the likelihood of being able to dance. Unravelling the problem is a partnership that suggests a mutuality in giving and receiving. The end result is unknown but unravelling can allow hope to draw close. In hope we find healing, rehabilitation, and entry back into *normal* living in ways that affirm

---

4. Stratford, *To Live Each Day*, 60.

2.1. Dancing God

relationships, the value of life, and possibilities for the re-establishment of familiar patterns that generate life. Herein lies the possibility for dancing.

A significant difficulty in interfaith conversation is an underlying desire among participants that the other would be more like them. Attitude is indeed a critical question in the field of pastoral care, a question that in its answering takes us back into the history of pastoral care. Remembering that pastoral care has its roots in the Hebrew scriptures, and is defined more extensively within the Christian church as "the care of souls," the question of how pastoral care might be carried out across faith boundaries requires in the answering some radical changes to our understanding of pastoral care, not least of which is an understanding of the working of faiths that differ. In a previous work[5] I laid claim to the necessity of rearticulating pastoral care in order to clearly understand that, while both spiritual care and religious care are contained under the umbrella of pastoral care, the most helpful expression of pastoral care within a pluralist society is found in spiritual care. Interfaith reality, however, dictates that pastoral engagement with the other must be undertaken as spiritual care.

The question of attitude towards other religions, raised by Kung in 1985, is of particular importance in our multicultural world. Within the Christian way, for example, we can still find comments such as "Jesus is the way" and "There is no salvation apart from Jesus," with the result that the claim of conversion to Christianity as an imperative still lies within its doctrines. This imperative finds its most strident expression within fundamentalist Christianity, in which all other religions are doomed, and even many Christian denominations are also doomed unless they walk the narrow path. Islamic fundamentalism, which considers all others as infidels, dooms all who do not wish to convert to Islam. A wider, more inclusive standpoint is always subverted by the noise of fundamentalism. Some years ago, in an exchange of emails arising from complaints, a man working as a chaplain was told that he must remember always that he was required to work within guidelines that included the need to acknowledge and affirm the faith of those—including non-Christians—who found nurture in their own faith journey; that is, to be hospitable. He replied, in an email resigning from his work as chaplain, in the following vein:

> The only place where faith is found is in God's message through the words of Christ. To say that Buddhism, or Islam or Hinduism has a rightness in its faith is saying that what Jesus has done on the

5. Stratford, "Study in the Re-Articulation of Pastoral Care," 2013.

> Cross is not enough . . . without belief in Jesus' redeeming work they are bound for Hell—we must not be afraid to say so, Jesus wasn't. We can still show the love, acceptance, and compassion of Christ while sharing with them that salvation is found nowhere else. . . . Do you think Jesus would espouse something other than the Christian faith?[6]

Opinions such as this, bankrupt of understanding of Christian teaching, judgemental about the nature of religious life as multifaceted, and nonsensical in the implication that Jesus the Jew was somehow a Christian, exacerbate tensions between groups.

This person's God is a no-risk God, one who does not dance but rather takes life very seriously. This respondent has a very serious idea about religious connection and therefore decries any possibility of a dancing God. The difficulty for this person, however, is that his notion of God bears no connection with reality; for who can decide who and what God does or wants?

Dancing is an expression of emotion that takes form in many ways. Dancing also contains risk. So we might ask: What risks did the dancing God take? Considering this, as we should, in the context of story, we may well respond that the risk was in the *making of people*. The stories suggest that from the very beginning God's risk was well founded in the desire of Adam and Eve for autonomy. To speak of a dancing God and a risk taker is not blasphemy, as some might claim, but a reality stemming from the life of people.

Traditionally however, Gods have been fearful beings, ready to punish any slight, more inclined to discipline than to compassion. Such a viewpoint is clearly a projection of followers and seems to indicate that this is their considered opinion. We appear to want to be more like the little man than the dancing figure. Any search for meaning, however, needs to be open to all possibilities.

Being in contact with a dancing God allows us the liberty to not take life earnestly, but take it as precious. A dancing God suggests joy and satisfaction over creation, over all things, over people. The story of creation in the Hebrew scriptures tells us that throughout creation God saw that it

---

6. Extracted from an email dated October 21, 2006, written in response to a statement about standards that chaplains were required to adhere to. The email was sent to the president of the Australian Health and Welfare Chaplains Association. The Association had at that time assembled a book of standards that government health departments throughout the country had received.

2.1. Dancing God

was good. Perhaps our response might be, "If it was good enough for God, it is good enough for us." A creation that is good must include people, and this is what the story tells us. A divine blessing on all creation claims our attention to a life in which we can acknowledge we can live with difference and choose to value others; we can dance with God.

The quality we find in spiritual care is linked to our concept of the divine in our life. The question that frequently needs to be challenged has to do with expectations. These include expectations of ourselves as we search for meaning, and we need to inquire about what meaning we want. I think we frequently search for results that are comforting and reinforce our selected image. If, however, we are seeking to direct our search for our own satisfaction, we are becoming like the little man who was focused on the ground, and a particular article, carefully wrapped in his cocoon, protected from everything going on outside. The little man has no desire to interact with the God who dances.

An engagement with spiritual care, however, is an engagement with the unknown, a venturing towards the dance. A primary function of spiritual care lies in its sense of journey through the unknown, and through unknowing towards understanding, and a determination to continue the journey. In this it may be said that windows are opened on wisdom.

2.2. Tell Them *I Am*

When, as written in the Exodus stories of the Hebrew scriptures, Moses was confronted in the desert with a vision of a burning bush and a demand for action, the name provided by the Hebrew God to Moses was *I Am*; not a name—a statement of *being*. Not good enough, replied Moses, saying to God, "If I come to the Israelites and say to them, 'The God of your ancestors has sent me to you,' and they ask me, 'What is his name?' what shall I say to them?" God said to Moses, "*I am who I am*." He said further, "Thus you shall say to the Israelites, '*I am* has sent me to you'" (Exod 3:13–15, emphasis added). Moses sought familiarity and comfort for himself and his people, but all had to be satisfied with this particular appellation. This god was not the property of the Hebrews, and could not be known to them by a particular and unique name. This god was not the Israelites' choice. The choosing was the other way round, grounded in their history. This was a god who simply was! No name. No ownership.

The response of this god to Moses' question established a difference. The people to whom Moses was to go with his message were expected to acknowledge two things. One was that they were dealing with the god of their ancestors. Having an ancestral god who recognized them removed some of the fears they may have had. Refusal to provide a name took this god out of the general milieu of gods, and required that the people acknowledge and trust. It was a statement about being, about presence. The demonstration of presence followed subsequently after Moses took up the challenge and returned to Egypt. It was then that this god became God for the Israelites. The Hebrew God, expressing "his" nature as *being*, opened pathways into being which all may share as they recognize and own their humanity.

2.2. Tell them *I Am*

Throughout history up to that point, religious attachments had always been to a god that could be named. In this way believers were able to recognize differences in the gods' natures and therefore respond accordingly. Classic examples of this are found in the Greek pantheon of divines. These include Aphrodite, goddess of love; Apollo, god of music; Ares, god of war; Hades, god of the underworld; Zeus, king of the gods, and many more, each having multiple responsibilities. Named and described by their followers, all knew their place and their tasks. All nations had their gods; cities also maintained gods. Individuals had their gods. Familiarity with and domestication of a god allowed for comfort and direct communication. Knowing who you were addressing provided some sense of security. Nevertheless, despite their familiarity, people lived with some trepidation amongst gods who were at times somewhat capricious in their responses.

Yet still, as Christians, we seek to name God. God is called "Father" and is addressed in such terminology as "Father God," "God the Father," and "Father of Jesus." Addressing God as our "Father" I think domesticates God. There is a familiarity and comfort in considering God in this way. Fatherhood means a *him*, so God very quickly became a *him*, and remains so. Such naming is a carryover from the early church and was continued and established thus by and in the church. Clergy figures became representatives of God and took on the designation of priests, bearing the title "Father."

As father figures, they were tasked with guidance and discipline of the faithful, and it all became rather autocratic. Rules, discipline, punishment, denial, exclusion—activities that can be recognized in the church through the centuries—still remain in elements of the Catholic Church, still considered by some as the true Christian church. Recognition appears to be less about being and more about authority. Authority requires—even demands—response. *Being* shares commonality. People and God have some things in common. The *being* of the Divine is apprehended in our breathing. Creation and sustainment are two of the aspects applied to God, and in the life-giving breaths we take the spirit of the Divine may be recognized.

Martin Heidegger, describing the process of conscious experience, claimed that it is a "letting what shows itself to be seen from itself, just as it shows from itself." He continues, "Being is to be grasped by means of the phenomenological method. However, being is always the being of a being, and accordingly it becomes accessible only indirectly through some existing entity."[1] Macquarrie offers some clarification: "As a matter of fact Heidegger has always been quite clear in his mind that *Being*, however we are to think of it, cannot be considered as a thing, another entity or something that is."[2] Not a thing, not an object; God cannot be named.

One constructive way to consider *being* is to associate it with presence. Through this entity of presence, which we can describe, some understanding of being will be possible. *Being* is contained in the words "*I Am*," and in our context of interfaith understanding, spiritual care is best described for our purposes as presence. Presence therefore becomes the way in which *being* may best be understood. Presence includes such descriptors as attendance, occurrence, incidence, existence, manifestation, and being there. *Being* therefore may be characterized by dignity, charisma, aura, authority, poise, air, bearing, comportment, and mien.

Being is frequently associated with empathy as a way of interaction with another. Ewert Cousins writes:

> I believe that we all have a capacity for empathy with another's spiritual values. I call this a 'shamanistic faculty'. In primal religions the shaman has the power to leave his body and travel to distant places, acquire knowledge, and return to pass this on to the community. In a similar fashion, in interreligious dialogue with our shamanistic faculty we can, as it were, leave our distinctive forms of consciousness and enter by way of empathy into the consciousness of others. In so doing we enter into their world of spiritual values—into their realm of faith—and experience this from the inside. Then we return enriched, bringing into our own world these values and a larger horizon of awareness.[3]

Entering into another's realm of faith is also entering into another's cultural expression of their faith. The culture in which one is nurtured falls naturally into a belief that it is better than the cultural experience of others. Values, norms, and mores become defining principles that reinforce the cultural suppositions. This spills over into religious belief, and indeed we can recognize a close link between the religion and cultural values of any given society. The risk of exclusivism is high and this frequently becomes visible in the attitude of majorities towards minorities.

---

1. Quoted in Korab-Karpowicz, "Martin Heidegger."
2. Macquarrie, *Martin Heidegger*, 4.
3 Cousins, *Nature of Faith*, 35.

2.2. Tell them *I Am*

Cultural differences are linked to history and geography, along with centuries of social change. Such variations also reflect variations in understanding of the sacred. Symbols and rituals reflect the cultures in which they developed, and none of these can be said to be a complete reflection of the sacred, nor can they be said to be the only valid responses to the sacred. That which is considered sacred in the lives of people, whatever name might be applied, is for that group the outcome of years—probably centuries—of experience.

Spiritual care encounters always run the risk of reaction to another's cultural response. It is clearly possible for potential culture clashes to occur during pastoral interactions. Pastoral visitors need always to remind themselves that they have a cultural history. Built-in attitudes become a considerable difficulty when culture, and its association with religion, is carried openly into spiritual care encounters. This is not to say that culture and religion should be hidden; rather, it says that if care is to be appropriately offered, culture and religion need to be subdued. As awareness grows, however, a more appropriate interaction will emerge, allowing for human encounter in which we may find a degree of commonality.

John Mabry in *Noticing the Divine*, writing from a spiritual direction perspective, reminds us of the many religious traditions in the world, each with something to add to spiritual understanding. He writes:

> As I reflected upon each of the world's traditions it struck me that although every religion addressed the same needs . . . each one was also distinctive, emphasizing different aspects of the spiritual life . . . the mythology of native traditions teaches us the value of telling our sacred stories; Taoism teaches us the importance of "not doing", learning to trust the Divine as the real spiritual guide; Judaism teaches us about the law and how to honour appropriate boundaries . . . each religion has a special gift to bestow.[4]

Everyone has a story to tell—some harrowing, some joyful—but always a story that comes from our inner being. In stories shared one may become aware of life as a precious gift.

Learning to trust the divine is a little more difficult than sharing a story. In everyday life there are many instances that involve trust. Some are inconsequential while others are important for our security and our life. Trusting a friend is a level of confidence most can reach. Reaching past this to an acknowledgement of beyondness is, for some, a step too far. For

---

4. Mabry, *Noticing the Divine*, vi.

Part Two: Spiritual Care—Bridging the Differences

others it is a step into relationship, and an apprehending of spirit presence. We find here, the is-ness of the divine.

Spiritual care, however hesitantly, needs to embrace stories and trust as essential elements in any search for meaning. Engaging in a mutual sharing of human *being* is a powerful expression of the ongoing search for meaning that will enable seekers to reach towards the essential nature of what it means to be human. Spiritual care also needs, particularly in the intimacies of sharing, to maintain boundaries that will allow for clarity in searching and understanding.

Stephen Prothero, concluding his analysis of a number of key religions, offers a short quote from Daoism: "'The Tao has ten thousand gates,' say the masters, and it is up to each one of us to find our own." He continues:

> To explore the great religions is to wander through these ten thousand gates. It is to enter into Hindu conversations on the logic of Karma and rebirth, Christian conversations on the mechanics of sin and resurrection, and Daoist conversations on flourishing here and now. . . . It is also to encounter rivalries between Hindus and Muslims in India, between Jews and Muslims in Israel, and between Christians and Yoruba practitioners in Nigeria. Each of these rivals offers a different vision of a 'human being fully alive.' . . . All their adherents are human beings . . . so each of these religions attends to our embodiment and to the human predicament, not least by defining what it is to be fully alive.[5]

This is surely the fundamental goal of any search for meaning in life. It is a search that needs dialogue in order to stretch across the boundaries that separate people into religious and culture groups. It is simply not enough to consider that meaning can be summed up as obedience to God and hope in a promise of future eternal life. Attaching this to the fundamental difficulties encountered in this life is clearly insufficient no matter what future hopes might be claimed. Cultural groups are the building blocks of life, but spiritual care can help people to see also that the building blocks for one group have the possibility of meshing with the building blocks of another group, enriching the experience of all.

Experience is enriched through relationship, and relationships begin with the knowing of a name. We all seek a name when we first meet somebody. Indeed, names are an essential part of who we are. We introduce someone or are introduced by someone through the name by which we

---

5. Prothero, *God Is Not One*, 333.

2.2. Tell them *I Am*

have become accustomed to owning as who we are. Without a name we become lost, and we are all aware of the distress that faces people when names are forgotten. The difficulty is that there is no other way in which we can immediately acknowledge another. It is possible, however, to begin to know another more slowly as we enter into relationship within. We would also agree that knowing a name does not equate with knowing the person. There is much in our life that a name can never reveal.

The *I Am* that God gave to Moses did not make matters clear for him, so God took it a step further: "I am the God of your ancestors" (Exod 3:15). Reaching back into history, Moses was able to establish links with what he knew. Abraham was an ancestor. Abraham figured in their life before Egypt. The *I Am* was an invitation to understand that this God continued in their lives. The *I Am* is a declaration of presence; it is not a title. We participate in that presence moment by moment as we breathe. The breath of God in creation is the breath of the spirit in our lives. All must therefore participate; breathing is the one constant for life. As we live, so we are, and *being* is an expression of us. In *being* we find meaning.

Moses' desert experience had ramifications far beyond his imagination. From his encounter the Israelite people were born. From disparate groups they coalesced into a people with one mind. It is all a long way from our experience of life, but we all from time to time have what we sometimes name as "desert experiences." By this we mean experiences that contain something of desolation and emptiness. Sometimes these leave us with feelings of hopelessness.

We may not have the same result that befell Moses, but we do have other possibilities available for our aid as we search for meanings from the desert. Our desert experiences, as with Moses, are spiritual experiences; deserts loom large in our scriptural accounts. The nature of deserts is such as to strip away the extras and show us the fundamentals of life. Desert discoveries may be valued as beginnings for a different way. Sharing this with another is part of the essence of spiritual care.

2.3. On *Being*, and Meeting the Sacred

TRADITIONALLY, PASTORAL CARE IN the church had its focus in religious care, which was recognized as care of the soul. The term "chaplain," originally custodian of the cloak of St. Martin,[1] emerged from the church's life particularly linked to soul care. Pastoral care was the establishment, in its practice, of a basis for ensuring the safe passage of believers through their Christian life—support for one's religious journey, or more simply, religious care. In our day, pastoral care must be recognized as having two aspects, one of which is religious care and the other spiritual care. The question that confronts us, therefore, is whether the validity of religious care for all who have an intervention with a chaplain can be sustained.

It is clear that in any multicultural and/or multifaith society, pastoral care must be more than religious care. Any one care provider will approach any activity of care from his/her own religious background, whatever that may be. Religious care only retains its validity when occurring within a religious framework in which both the offerer and receiver of care participate. The only alternative to this will be when a specific request might be made, and even then care will need to be exercised to avoid any sense of overstepping boundaries.

In life, religious understanding is fostered and sustained through the religious institution. The collective gathering for prayer and worship is most important in maintaining religious viewpoints. In the gathering,

1. The story is a long one. Briefly, as a soldier Martin met a freezing beggar, and, cutting his cloak in half, he gave half to the beggar. That night he dreamed, and in his dream heard Jesus speak about him as "the one who clad me." The cloak was miraculously restored, and eventually preserved as a relic. The Latin word *capella* (short cloak) was extended to the people charged with preserving the cloak. They were the *cappellani* or chaplains. http://www.religionfacts.com/martin-tours.

the individuals come together of their own volition to share their religious experience. Part of this sharing is found in the liturgy, the patterns for worship with which people are familiar, and also in the symbols that gather thoughts and emotions to focus on the sacred.

The familiarity that encourages ongoing commitment to a life of faith is fostered through religious symbols and rituals along with social and cultural expressions of daily life. Expressions of faith life differ markedly from each other. These differences certainly have an impact on attempts at religious care but may also be a limiting factor in spiritual care. It all depends on the approach taken by the one offering spiritual care, and we all need to acknowledge our own attitudes and biases. A word from Robert Runcie is most pertinent to this process:

> We need both courage and humility to recognize the work of the spirit among us in other faiths. It takes courage to acknowledge religious diversity as a rich spiritual resource, rather than a cause for competition and tension. And it takes humility and sincerity to concede that there is a certain incompleteness in each of our traditions. However diverse in their development and message, they always remain in a process of becoming, so that there is always room for growth towards a fuller, richer version of the truth.[2]

It is important in all spiritual care interactions in which we encounter a different faith stance that we remain focused on the task of unravelling, and do not anticipate that we will be able to reach towards a common understanding of truth that encompasses both points of view, therefore placing the combined truth as superior to individual truth. A more inclusive interaction will lead the carer and one receiving care to the acceptance that both truths are valid. A spiritual care encounter, however, is not in order to agree about truths; it is in order to explore life stories. Peter Speck says of spiritual care that it

> will depend on the patient and the care giver being willing to enter together into the experience and explore without quite knowing where it will lead. The uncertainty which this embraces can be challenging for both, but especially so for the pastoral care giver if he or she has not explored ultimate or existential issues in their own life story.[3]

---

2. Runcie, *Many Mansions*, 25.
3. Speck, *Spiritual Care in Health Care*, 21.

Part Two: Spiritual Care—Bridging the Differences

The challenge for all seeking to provide spiritual care lies in self-understanding along with a commitment to *being*. The integrity of care may be visible in uprightness, honesty, and sincerity, but may be breached through an inability to maintain what the dictionary says of integrity as "the condition of having no part or element wanting; completeness, soundness."[4] In Chesterton's *The Man Who Was Thursday* we discover Syme protesting a lack of integrity because in life there is a strong tendency to see only "the back of the world." Such a way of seeing does not allow for completeness and soundness. "Everything is stooping and hiding a face," says Syme. What is needed is a different way of looking at living. "If we could only get round in front."[5]

Any sense of our own being must necessarily contain an understanding of life and living. All people have their own life to live and must therefore continually adjust to the ever-shifting context in which they develop their own way of life. Everyone of us needs also to understand and acknowledge that the fundamental essence of being lies in the fact that we breathe. Only in the context of this activity can we become aware of life and engage in reflection on the wholeness of who we are. The image of breathing is discovered in the *Dictionary of Biblical Imagery*, linked to the Hebrew expression that also encompasses wind and spirit. "Breath is part of a group of words, including wind and spirit that evoke a wide range of dynamic relationships between God, humanity and creation. Hebrew *ruah* can mean: *breath, wind, or spirit*, allowing more than one interpretation of many Old Testament passages."[6]

In the very beginning of our life, and essential to it, we catch our breath in order to begin living. There are also times in our life when we become somewhat lost and disorientated. It is then that we need to take stock and review the things that are impacting our life. Spiritual care assists in the catching of breath, which is how we describe stopping to consider something. Catching our breath provides the impetus to re-enter our life. The element of the earth's life that we describe as atmosphere contains all that is necessary for physical life. Indeed, this particular atmosphere that surrounds and enfolds us is essential for our life. Without it we cannot live and any change in its composition will threaten our life. Spiritual care recognizes the intimacy between breath and wind and spirit and finds in

4. Little et al., *Shorter Oxford English Dictionary*, 1088.
5. Chesterton, *Man Who Was Thursday*, 132.
6. Ryken et al., *Dictionary of Biblical Imagery*, 119.

2.3. On *Being*, and meeting the Sacred

any exploration a sacred link, in the presence of which conversation may enter new depths of understanding. The life present in the atmosphere that surrounds us enters into the very depths of our being as we breathe, and provides the essential ingredient for daily living. Spiritual care, in its search for meaning, takes place in the atmosphere of life. It can also be said that spiritual care takes place in an ambiance that is potentially life-threatening. Searching for meaning reduces that potential.

The gifts that flow from engagement in deep spiritual care are avenues to understanding that have the potential to link all people of all faiths with the spirituality inherent in their faith. At the core of all the religious expressions of believers lies a sense of otherness, of beyondness, of being, of the sacred. The notion of the sacred needs to be understood as a valid expression of relationship no matter what name is applied to the faith being followed. One question that needs to be considered, therefore, is that of the meaning of *sacred*. Sacred, as an action, is variously defined as: "Someone who is *exclusively devoted to a deity or to some religious ceremony or use*; Something or someone who is *worthy of or regarded with reverence and awe*; Some thing or activity that is *connected with or intended for religious use*."[7]

Mircea Eliade claims that "the sacred reveals itself." Definitions therefore are of limited value. It is more likely that, rather than define *sacred*, we experience the sacred. In revealing itself, says Eliade, the sacred "provides a fixed point from which we may orient our life."[8] We might well add that spiritual care is a process that helps that orientation. In part three of this book we will become aware of elements of spirituality that will provide us with links to our experience of the sacred.

It can be demonstrated that adherents to all faith expressions can lay claim to a sacred relationship within their religious attachment. When, however, one has a strong relationship with the sacred and practices this in company with like-minded others, the temptation to defend the group's position vis-à-vis other groups is strong. Frequently there is a superiority claimed over those who seek a personal relationship with the sacred but don't practice this within an identifiable group. It is also clear that among individual seekers after the sacred, even if associated with a group, any belief claims are clearly diverse in their application. This therefore requires that spiritual care, acknowledging the truth of the sacred in the individual's life, does not engage with the sacred but with the person.

---

7. Makins et al., *Collins Concise Dictionary*, 1180.
8. Eliade, *Sacred and Profane*, 11, 21.

Part Two: Spiritual Care—Bridging the Differences

If one is to offer adequate and relevant spiritual care, a first requirement is some understanding of spirituality and its impact on one's own life. We cannot know the other's understanding until conversation is engaged. That engagement must be informed by our own understanding, and the next chapter seeks to make this clear.

2.4. Listening

IN THE *Shorter Oxford Dictionary*, the meanings attached to *listen* are, firstly, "to concentrate on hearing something," and, secondly, "to take heed; pay attention."[1] Listening is a basic skill in interpersonal communication. In this twenty-first century, however, much communication does not require the physical act of listening. The bulk of interpersonal communication happens through emails and mobile phone messaging. Communication in our day, therefore, is far more visual than in previous years. Commercial television exploits the visual impact through the action and repetition of adverts, all of which are put into place by those who plan the advertising programme. Words and pictures are both used but in most instances the words are secondary to the picture and are at times superfluous. Repetition ensures that the picture, and therefore the article being advertised, is implanted in the mind of the viewer.

Many programmes are based on a supposition of a minimal attention span, and are broken into small segments among the adverts. Programmes themselves do not rely on a great deal of dialogue, but make up for it with lots of explicit action. Regular interruptions for advertising result in people actually stopping listening. Listening is a declining skill. Shorthand message conversations via telephone do not require one to listen, but simply to respond to the recorded message. Social outings in clubs that shout noise are, as a result, devoid of conversation, avoiding the need to listen. Sustained attention is not possible, nor in many cases considered desirable. How then can we hear and so respond to those in need?

We listen to something or someone in order to hear, so clearly we need to pay attention to what is making the sounds or being said. Deep and

1. Onions, *Shorter Oxford Dictionary*, 1222.

concentrated listening will hear at different levels. Margaret Mohrmann writes of "paying attention to those who suffer, hearing their pain seeing their damaged selves . . . means, more than anything, listening to the stories they have to tell us."[2] Patricia Butler, in *Reflections on Living While Dying*, on learning that cancer had assailed her, wrote of her "world turned upside down—absolutely shattered!"[3] It was the deep-down response to the disease that had stopped her life in its tracks. It is a story of damaged faith, and of despair. It is a story crying out for understanding. It is the beginning of an uncertain journey through illness with endurance and courage. It is a story that requires concentrated and sensitive listening. Listening is one part of a conversation, and as we engage with another the quality of the listening will open doors into another's needs, and enable the dialogue to enter deeper levels of need not previously visible. Listening, however, may also take us beyond one another into a stance that begins to hear the whole world.

One of the stories in *Tales of a Magic Monastery* contains the following reflection of a monk who ventured deep into a cave. On this journey he listens.

> Finally I began to hear a rumbling sound, like mighty waters. You know what it was? It was the tears of the whole world! I heard the bitter tears of *everyone's* fear, hurt, despair, disappointment, rage. Everyone's. And I heard the sweet tears too—you know, when you're loved, when you're safe at last, a loved one restored, those tears of joy.[4]

This is a story, a fantasy that offers a glimpse into the difficulties that surround people every day. The monk in the story has been granted a second chance to return from death to life and find some meaning for himself and for others. The cave is the mythological pathway into the centre of the earth, and his travels result in him hearing the things previously unheard.

There is a desperate need for good listening as political, social, and religious groups grab hold of opportunities and begin to use them to their own advantage, which then disadvantages others. People have slipped into violence. Wars thus begun continue and many are killed. Thousands are now fleeing in fear. The tragedy in all this is that no one is listening. On the one hand there is a determination to establish a religious state. On the other

---

2. Mohrmann, *Paying Attention*, 65.
3. Butler, *Reflections on Living*, 4.
4. Theophany, *Tales of a Magic Monastery*, 27.

hand there is a determination to prevent this. Both sides resort to violence to achieve their end. The cries of the afflicted ones in the middle are largely ignored. In this massive disruption in the lives of the populace the hidden effects emerge as fear, hunger, loss, general violence, harm, and much more. We must all listen if from country to country tradition, custom, and social harmony are to prevail.

Taking time to listen provides time for the sharing of concerns, differences in understanding, and for recognition of the deep attachments people have to many aspects of their lives. Careful and focused listening introduces us to qualities of life otherwise not visible. In the practice of spiritual care, focused listening is enhanced by the quality of presence. Presence is an investment of time and energy—an investment of self. A presence such as this is not caught up with a need to do something. It is content to be. Wolterstorff writes out of his grief:

> If you think your task as comforter is to tell me that really, all things considered, it's not so bad, you do not sit with me in my grief but place yourself off in the distance. . . . I need to hear from you that you are with me in my desperation. To comfort me, you have to come close. Come sit beside me on my mourning bench.[5]

The kind of listening that is able to hear the grief of loss will not be in a hurry to do and say things of little value. Listening appropriately will allow for the invitation to come and sit with the other in difficulty.

There is more, for listening is not only to be done with ears, nor is it only focused on another in trouble. If one is to help another in the search for meaning, one has to also listen to one's own quest. Part of that listening concerns the divine. We do not have to wear a religious label but we do have to seek out for ourselves that which holds us together and enables meaningful living. This is a journey into awareness, and requires us to walk a pathway that will lead to that awareness. The first step lies in choosing the path on which we will be comfortable. We may, of course, already be on that path, simply needing to see it a little more clearly.

The very word "spiritual" in spiritual care implies some connection with the sacred, and we will make this link more clearly in part three of this book. Sacred ikons, sacred writings, sacred places, and sacred spaces all have their place within sacred journeys. Different faith groups have different understandings of the sacred; in listening we will develop understanding

---

5. Wolterstorff, *Lament for a Son*, 34.

Part Two: Spiritual Care—Bridging the Differences

and acceptance. Shrines also are places of pilgrimage for many. Throughout this country there are a myriad of shrines, big and small, to remind us of sacred presence in the loss of life among those who went to war. Throughout the world shrines exist and are gathering places where people seek out the sacred. I am mindful of a journey I made as a young boy with my mother at the end of World War II to the Shrine of Remembrance in Melbourne, Australia. Thousands attended to reflect on the previous years, to give thanks for the present, and no doubt to reflect on the future.

To make a journey to many of these shrines is impossible for most. To attempt to sit near many shrines in order to listen in a sacred ambience is not realistic. We may need a different journey to encounter our own sacred ambience. One helpful way lies in walking a labyrinth. Lauren Artress writes of labyrinths as:

> Divine imprints with universal patterns most likely created in the collective unconscious, birthed through the human psyche and passed down through the ages. Labyrinths are mysterious because we do not know the origin of their design, or exactly how they provide space that allows clarity. A labyrinth is not a maze with its blind alleys and traps. There is only one way in and one way out, and as it twists and turns, we are guided through all points of the compass and phases of the moon until we reach the centre. The path may mirror the path through life, sometimes seeming lost, sometimes seeming to go backwards, but always the point ahead remains the same.[6]

There are many labyrinths in existence throughout the world, and an exploration of the Internet will locate one near you. My initial journey occurred at Grace Cathedral whilst on holiday in San Francisco.

Sometimes, however, religious formats become labyrinths of a more puzzling kind. Listening is clearly an important element in worship practices. The labyrinth of engagement with rituals may become a puzzle when too many words are used. Parishioners are expected to listen and understand, but multitudes of words do not always make the way clear. Failing to hear and understand that to which we are listening can result in missing the point, and even becoming stranded in the labyrinth. It is even more problematic if we are trying to understand a different faith standpoint more clearly.

---

6. Artress, *Labyrinths, Sacred Space*, 76.

2.4. Listening

Of particular value in the framework of spiritual care, taking heed and paying attention are the attributes of listening that are most important for our understanding. Listening, we recognize the deep hurts and needs of others, and begin also to recognize that there is something of a sacred trust evolving with the story. It is therefore important for the authenticity of the care we offer that we find and then travel on the pathways that take us towards our own understanding of the sacred in our lives.

Whatever the shape of our faith standpoint might be, we can all find value and insight in the links we have with those objects sacred for us, or in the walking we might do on paths that lift our spirits. We do not seek the *oohs* and *aahs* of contentment in the garden, beautiful as it may be. The paths we need to walk along to discover some wisdom in our listening are like the labyrinth: ways in a journey with a destination. Spiritual care is in some ways a two-way journey. On the one hand the one receiving care tells a story that begins a journey to understanding meanings. On the other hand the one we might call the carer discovers a road that s/he also must travel; the destination an encounter with the sacred.

2.5. Meditation

WHAT HAS MEDITATION TO do with spiritual care? Spiritual care is a focused activity, aimed at helping another along the journey towards meaning. As such it embraces a wide spectrum of attachments and attitudes, some of which may need refining along the way. Any focused activity drains energy. Meditation assists in replacing that energy. This chapter focuses on three of the synonyms attached to meditation—*contemplation*, *reflection*, and *musing*, as a way of helping our understanding of energy replacement. In many ways we all meditate from time to time on matters that concern us. Some of this we might call musing, a reflective, thoughtful contemplation about something or someone we may be worried about or some happening or relationship that gave us joy, and many matters in between.

Meditation may take the form of a quiet conversation with another. The other may be someone you are familiar and comfortable with, so that together you are able to share some deep concerns. The other may be the one who provides the elements of sacredness in your life, one whom you might name in ways that provide meaning for you in your spiritual life. Karl Rahner's *Encounters with Silence*, for example, is a series of meditations on God. It is claimed as "one of the most lucid and loving of his works" and a "book of prayerful reflections."[1] Meditation may become a time of silence, of being still and allowing thoughts to emerge and grow.

Meditation has global roots among a number of religious traditions. Two of these will suffice for the purposes of this work. One is framed in the Christian church; the other is framed in Eastern, particularly Asian

---

1. From the back cover of the 1958 edition of *Encounters with Silence*.

religious traditions. Together they are representative of a considerable portion of the world's population.

In the Christianity of the West meditation comes to us out of the Catholic tradition, and for a long time was only recognizable in that tradition. The Reformation, which ultimately spawned a plethora of denominations, neglected meditation in favor of prayer and proclamation. To a large extent this is still so today.

Morton Kelsey is described as a theologian, psychologist, educator, priest, and man of prayer, and his book *The Other Side of Silence* reflects all of these. For Kelsey, meditation is the prime method for encountering the divine, and that for him means God. Much of what he writes, however, will resonate with all who seek to find a quiet reflective space. He says:

> Where meditation is concerned, we need to realize two things. Meditation is simple and natural, like a seed growing and becoming a tree. At the same time it requires the right conditions, conditions not provided by the secular world today. If meditation is to touch reality, we must seek out the right climate.[2]

Spiritual care clearly contains an association with the divine. A need for reflection, therefore, arising out of an interfaith encounter, will not seek simply to analyze the conversation, although this may at times be helpful. Meditation will take note of meanings, will reflect on the journey, will travel slowly and allow the encounter to creep into awareness.

Engaging in meditation allows for a review, not only of the conversation, but also of the way the carer offered spiritual care. Contemplation allows for an inspection of what has transpired. In the context of spiritual care it is important to observe and survey the process undertaken in the interaction. Only by putting our behavior under scrutiny will we become more clear and intentional about spiritual care. Only by scrutinizing what occurred will we find our strengths and weaknesses and be able to attach value to them. After all the goal of spiritual care is to assist another to consider the difficulties, and the joys, of a journey towards meaning. Sitting still and contemplating the process of care, along with the insights gained by the carer and the one receiving care, is glimpsing the growing edges of such journeys.

Meditation, as well as being a time of stillness and listening, is also a time for reflection. In this we hold up a mirror, as it were, and consider as

---

2. Kelsey, *Other Side of Silence*, 32.

we look the things that occurred during the spiritual care interaction. In our mind's eye we can visualize the images that emerge, recognizing their value, or not. Musing on the process and content, we find a variety of small happenings that bring the interaction to life again in our quiet and thoughtful time. These can absorb our interest and allow us to find many elements of meaning that might otherwise have escaped us. This is not a time for making judgements, nor about grading the usefulness of the conversation. It is simply to allow us to relive moments and expressions. We are not to dismiss the differences. Meditation is a pathway to awareness, and as such may be a way for spiritual grounding. Meditation need not always be solitary. Musing with a supervisor, for example, can be a helpful process and should not be decried.

Meditation is a time to ponder, to give thorough or deep consideration. Our pondering can take us deeper into the interaction and discover the presence of mystery. Meaning in life is a search undertaken by many for millennia. For some the search was never completed and they were forever unsatisfied. The mystery of meaning, however, may in fact lie in the search rather than attainment. Searching and gathering insight results, we might claim, in meaning for the moment. But as long as life continues searching will continue, building on what has gone before. Pondering this may not result in any conclusion except to recognize that the search itself is of value, and that ultimate meaning may not be attainable.

Our musings can be informed and enhanced by one such as Hildegard of Bingen. Gabriele Uhlein, in the introduction to her book *Hildegard of Bingen*, writes of Hildegard's spiritual grounding:

> While oneness is indeed a mystic theme of Hildegard's, she does not superficially dismiss differences and polarities. She dares to depict the human being in truth, as creator and created; as gracious, compassionate and loving; but also as destroyer and destroyed, as malicious, obstinate and self-indulgent. Further, the good and the bad, the light and the dark are recognized as ever present in a multitude of forms, hues and aromas for our senses to perceive. Hildegard makes it quite clear that to be human is to choose, to respond with awareness, to discern, and to act accordingly.[3]

Spiritual care is never only about the other person. The carer is also an active participant in any interaction, bringing his or her own truth into the conversation. Spiritual care is never about one providing guidance to

---

3. Uhlein, *Hildegard of Bingen*, 15.

2.5. Meditation

another. There needs to be a mutuality in any spiritual care interaction, as from the sharing each discovers new dimensions of meaning. Meditation arising from a particular event must take account of the wholeness that Hildegard presents.

The dictionary defines meditation as thinking deeply of spiritual matters.[4] Coming from a spiritual care interaction, it is appropriate therefore to take time to think about the interaction. It is also an appropriate time to refrain from thinking, allowing the interaction to speak to you as you listen. It does require some concentration, hence the value in finding quiet space—even sacred space in which to be still. The sacred space in which the prophet Elijah found himself makes an important point for our own attempts at being still. Elijah was a prophet who not only prophesied doom on apostate rulers but also was God's instrument in their total destruction. The result was that those who were left sought to kill him. He ran away and ended up in southern Judea, in a cave on what was known as the Holy Mountain. There he heard a voice telling him to stand outside the cave and wait for God to pass by:

> Now there was a great wind, so strong that it was splitting mountains and breaking rocks in pieces before the Lord, but the Lord was not in the wind; and after the wind an earthquake, but the Lord was not in the earthquake; and after the earthquake a fire, but the Lord was not in the fire; and after the fire a sound of sheer silence. (1 Kgs 19:11–12)

The story continues and tells us that the silence was in effect God speaking to Elijah. Meditation is listening to the silence, not to the noise.

We have been considering meditation from a particular perspective in which there is a long history of mysticism, and the processes of contemplation and the introspective life. Meditation is also found among many whose motivation lies outside all traditional religions, and claims the attention of large numbers of people throughout the world. There are many who take time for silence as they seek ways to relocate their lives away from busyness to a special place in the hills or on the beach; for some the desert is such a place. Starhawk writes of earth-based spirituality as a foundation for meditation: "Unless our spiritual practice is grounded in real connection to the natural world, we run the risk of simply manipulating our own internal imagery and missing the real communication taking place all around us."[5]

---

4. Little et al., *Shorter Oxford English Dictionary*, 1300.
5. Starhawk, *Earth Path*, 11.

Kosuke Koyama, in his early book *50 Meditations*, writes of his visit to the Shwe Dagon Pagoda in what was then Rangoon. Requirements included taking off one's shoes some distance from the pagoda, necessitating a slow walk on rough ground. Reflecting on this experience, he says, "That which is holy must be approached slowly."[6] On his second visit he discovered that a lift had been installed to get visitors quickly to the top. Meditation is not travelling by lift. It is approaching slowly. Meditation, travelling slowly, enables us to see something more than the ordinary.

Meditation plays a significant part in the Hindu and Buddhist traditions. Jayaram V, in his essay "Dhyana or Meditation in Hindu Tradition," explains that: "The purpose of meditation or *dhyana* is to become consciously aware of or investigate into one's own mind and body to know oneself. It is essentially an exclusive as well as an inclusive process in which one withdraws one's mind and senses from the distraction of the world and contemplates upon a chosen object or idea with concentration."[7]

Information from the Internet informs us further that "Buddhist meditation is a form of mental concentration that leads ultimately to enlightenment and spiritual freedom. Meditation occupies a central place in all forms of Buddhism, but has developed characteristic variations in different Buddhist traditions."[8]

Venerable Master Chin Kung tells us in his *Collected Works* that the core of the Buddha's teaching "contains three major points: discipline, meditation, wisdom. Wisdom is the goal and deep meditation or concentration is the crucial process toward achieving wisdom."[9] Master Chin further tells us that the goal of Buddhist teaching is the "mind of sincerity, purity, equality, compassion and awakening."[10] Only with this mind, he claims, will we be able to solve all problems.

---

6. Koyama, *50 Meditations*, 9.
7. http://www.hinduwebsite.com/hinduism/essays/meditation.asp
8. http://www.religionfacts.com/meditation/buddhism
9. Chin Kung, *Collected Works*, 7.
10. Ibid., 548.

2.6. Presence

IN ORDER THAT SPIRITUAL care be an adequate and helpful encounter, there needs to be a strong and inclusive sense of presence. John O'Donohue explains presence as both a deep desire and mysterious being: "Presence is something you sense, and you know, but cannot grasp."[1] One attendant meaning for presence is company, and from company we can move to companionship. From here the next step can take us to a deeper sense of belonging to each other. Mutual belonging is a deeply spiritual relationship that reaches below mere acquaintance to discover a spiritual presence representative of the divine. Spiritual care that exudes presence is true companionship, and the carer and receiver of care belong together. Such belonging becomes an affirmation of religious attachments and a valuing of them, and is itself an assurance that all religious connections have their own validity.

Concluding her study on the ministry of presence, Janet Stokes draws a comparison between the presence of the pastoral visitor, the presence of that which is holy, and the less than helpful visiting for a chat:

> Ministry of presence and presence of the Spirit are both viable, although somewhat separate, realities occurring during pastoral visitation. Ministry of presence is clearly defined by patients more in the sense of accompanying the patient in distress than in "passing the time of day." . . . perhaps pastoral care givers might stop using the phrase "ministry of presence" to refer to shallow visitation, and instead recognize such shallowness for what it is more likely to be: a visit that does not bring or reveal the power of the Spirit, for a variety of reasons. . . . Then we could reserve "ministry

---

1. O'Donohue, *Eternal Echoes*, 55.

of presence" to refer to more graced and mutually experienced ministry.[2]

Many Christian providers of care enter a pastoral visit with the belief that the interaction will be guided by the Holy Spirit. While not intending to diminish the belief of the provider, there is a risk, particularly when encountering one from a different faith stance, of assuming that others will also become aware of the presence of the Holy Spirit. One of the outcomes of projecting one's own particular beliefs onto another, either overtly or by implication, is that presence will be obstructed. Hindering presence for the sake of one's faith stance will, however, also impede the spiritual care being offered. Spiritual care by its very nature seeks to be open to possibilities for the discovery of meaning that is true for the receiver. If prevented, the meaning that is sought will be tarnished by the meanings offered through the provider's belief. Whether the divine is present or not is a matter for discernment by the one seeking and receiving spiritual care. It must always be remembered that there are a multitude of opinions about the nature of the one Christians name as God.

Much has been written in Christian literature related to the presence of God, many of them devotional books. Two examples are Harakas,[3] a devotional book for Orthodox Christians, and Foster and Smith, who say in their introduction: "Genuine devotional writings . . . seek to touch the heart, to address the will, to mold the mind."[4] This sense of God's presence, interpreted in a number of ways, has guided, and continues to guide, Christians as an expression of their belief.

Chaplains with a background of Christianity, engaged to provide spiritual care, carry as we all do an understanding of God's presence with them. This understanding will almost certainly spill over into interactions between chaplains and patients, hence the need for caution. The question, therefore, that confronts us all is the way in which those engaging in spiritual care might interpret their particular understanding of divine presence as a model for establishing and maintaining presence in a pastoral encounter. This in turn raises the further question about what presence actually means. Clearly, presence may be expressed in a variety of ways. John Macquarrie, for example, in *Paths in Spirituality* identifies a key feature of Celtic spirituality as an "intense sense of presence." Macquarrie continues:

2. Stokes, *Ministry of Presence*, 198.
3. Harakas, *Through the Year with the Church Fathers*, 1984.
4. Foster et al., *Devotional Classics*, 1.

2.6. Presence

"The sense of God's immanence in his creation was so strong in Celtic spirituality as to amount sometimes almost to a pantheism. Of course, Celtic Christianity was continuous with the earlier Celtic paganism."[5]

O'Donohue takes this sense a little further, identifying presence as awareness of wholeness, embracing all things, all understandings, all feelings, as a way of balance in life: "In order to keep our balance we need to hold the interior and exterior, visible and invisible, known and unknown, temporal and eternal, ancient and new, together. . . . This wholeness is holiness."[6] In all this, balance is maintained through awareness in which the spirit is also active.

Purnell makes a further claim that "conversation that grows creatively . . . requires an alert presence and disciplined observation."[7] Presence is intimately connected with particular behavior, in which we find quietness, preparedness to suspend time, determination to stay as long as required, being still, listening carefully, and minimum talk.

Presence is frequently best understood through story. Sandy Engel tells of some visits at a time when circumstances were dire. One visitor was a family therapist whom she knew well. "He came to visit one day and asked if I wanted to go for a walk outside." They walked in silence for a time, and eventually she began to recognize the reality of what was happening:

> Amazingly, James still didn't verbally respond; but he gave me a big hug and let me cry. He neither validated my conclusion nor corrected me—leaving it to me to decide how I was going to "explain" this . . . how I was going to make sense of it. He let me reach my own conclusion while being completely present and supportive.[8]

William Avery writes on understanding the ministry of presence. Referring to the writing of philosopher Gabriel Marcel, Avery says:

> Marcel points out that presence is not identical with physically being present or attentiveness. A person may be close enough to touch, yet one may feel strongly that the person is not present. A person may be an attentive and conscientious listener and yet may give the impression of not being present, because that person cannot make room internally for the other. The person providing

---

5. Macquarrie, *Paths in Spirituality*, 122–23.
6. O'Donohue, *Anam Cara*, 14.
7. Purnell, *Conversation as Ministry*, 47
8. Engels, *Tale of Three Visits*, 2.

a presence must offer the whole self. If that does not occur, the person can only offer a temporary loan of resources.[9]

Karen Webb writes of her experiences as a pastor, and the difficulties she had visiting parishioners in hospital. Experiencing depths of gratitude, she began to rethink the value of what she had been doing:

> The strange thing was that, as time went on, I needed to be with people when they were hurting. I no longer stayed with them because "that is what pastors do," but because I cared about them. There was something about being fully present with my people that was closely connected to my sense of vocation, but I could not quite name it.[10]

As a pastor, Webb links her own developing understanding of presence with her understanding of God's presence in the following way: "They needed someone they could trust to listen while they worked through making difficult decisions, someone who could understand, someone who cared, someone to assure them of God's love."[11]

Presence, this sixth element of spiritual care, has to do with companioning another. To do so requires an investment of time and energy. Companioning is most important for healing. In companioning the spiritual care received is more than words, more than thinking about possibilities, more than drawing attention to meanings. It is fundamentally a *being with*. Companioning is a window into trust, listening, understanding, and caring, each of which contains essential elements of presence. The companion may be seen by some as revealing, simply by presence, even the deeper possibilities of spirit presence and its interpretation by the one receiving care as a loving God.

Spiritual care does not anticipate this as a necessary outcome of any pastoral interaction, nor is there an assumption about the nature of any belief expressed. It is always possible, perhaps even likely, that different faith standpoints will be encountered. The provider of care will be aware of the needs being expressed by the receiver and act accordingly. When these needs are addressed through attention to what is being expressed by the one receiving care, healing will be more likely. People will then feel well

---

9. Avery, *Understanding of Ministry of Presence*, 346–47.
10. Webb, *Pastoral Identity*, 78.
11. Ibid., 79.

2.6. Presence

served as their stories are heard, their belief validated, and the provider recognized as being truly present in the encounter.

The stories we have heard all indicate the proximity of one who cared. The caring, while undertaken differently, maintains for the one receiving care the strong sense of closeness and caring, or in different words, the presence of the other. In what way, therefore, might we consider "an invisible spirit felt to be nearby"?[12]

Backtracking to an earlier chapter, we are reminded of the Genesis story and the link established between wind, breath, and spirit. Wind is invisible. We are aware of its presence. We see signs of its presence. We can even see where it has been. This invisibility of the wind suggests the invisibility of the spirit. Recalling the affinity between wind and spirit put forward by the ancients who composed the story allows us to dismiss any notion of ghosts as a distraction. The story draws us towards holy presence, and its intimate link with life, in the breaths that we take from the time of our birth to the time of our dying. Between these events we share breath with all other living creatures. Between these events we are always in the presence of the holy. Spiritual care, at its best, engages with this presence, opening a gate through which the carer, receiver of care, and spirit may enter and encounter each other. Elie Wiesel reminds us, in a final word on spiritual care:

> In the face of suffering, one has no right to turn away, not to see. In the face of injustice, one may not look the other way. When someone suffers, and it is not you, that someone comes first. Another's very suffering gives him/her priority. . . . To watch over one who grieves is more urgent duty than to think of God.[13]

Suffering and injustice are rife in the world today. While suffering is not always due to injustice, what we are mindful of is that there is considerable injustice and many suffering as a result, fleeing their homes to find a better place. Presence is not often the human face they encounter. Refugees are not wanted, and the tendency is for countries to allow them through but refuse admittance. The world is becoming more isolationist as countries withdraw their presence and move people along. The more urgent duty is seen to be protecting the borders. Let others look after their needs.

---

12. Makins, *Collins Concise Dictionary*, 1057.
13. Wiesel, in Fox, *Original Blessing*, 286.

PART THREE

Spirituality—Recipe and Ingredients

Writing the Recipe

THE PRACTICE OF SPIRITUAL care requires from the practitioner an understanding of the meaning that might be attached to spirituality. This requires a consideration of the word "spiritual," which is defined as relating to the spirit or soul, and not to physical nature or matter. This is now too narrow a definition in a society that recognizes a more holistic view of people. We can no longer, in our time, hold sensibly to the dualism of soul and body. Tacey writes of a "new interest in the reality of spirit and its healing effects on life. It is our secular society realizing that it has been running on empty, and has to restore itself at a deep primal source."[1]

The definition fits a traditional Christian understanding of spiritual but cannot be applied to the wider claims of spirituality occurring across a range of religious standpoints. Spirituality is a quality of living that I would claim to be demonstrable in people's lives, despite a complete lack of any hard definition of its nature. Spirituality, generally recognized as a qualitative expression of relationship with the sacred, must be associated with the whole of life. It cannot be claimed as a possession, and indeed has no meaning if only linked to the religious terminology of "spirit" and "soul." There is also, in the practice of spiritual care, a requirement that spirituality

---

1. Tacey, *The Spirituality Revolution*, 1.

be addressed in all religious formulations, and not be limited to any one faith group. Our initial definition does not fit all religions.

Spirituality has its roots in the interaction between people and the sacred. Spirituality, therefore, cannot be possessed as one might, for example, possess a book; it is ours as a gift indissolubly linked to life itself. As with all gifts, however, some unwrapping is needed in order to come closer to the core nature of the gift, found in the way this gift is lived, with some of the possible outcomes of such living. Karen Lebacqz and Joseph Driskill, in *Ethics and Spiritual Care*, make the point that "Spirituality is seen as an element in human nature, frequently a depth-dimension of human existence. This approach considers spirituality to consist in human authenticity, self-transcendence, and the experiential dimension of human existence."[2]

Spirituality is not a feel-good activity; it is not about goodness, niceness, earth consciousness and so on. It is also not necessarily linked to religion, or church, or doctrine. Spirituality necessarily attaches to Spirit, and Spirit has links with that which is deemed sacred. Previously, dictionary definitions of the word "sacred" were considered, and we were able to see religious links that portray ways in which one might be recognized as being in touch with spirituality. The connection of spirituality with the sacred means, in general religious parlance, a connection with God. In most religious expressions in the world, people naturally speak of their god, even though there may be some differences in understanding. The important common factor is that spirituality, however defined, is connected to that which is deemed to be sacred. Spirituality, therefore, is quite special in the lives of people.

Stories of the gods come from many sources, and from many times, arising out of the experiences of culturally different people. Despite their differences, however, all express desires, hopes, and fears in the spirits who embrace them with a life that lifts them beyond the mundane. Spirituality has its beginnings in creation, more specifically, in the myths that have grown out of beliefs.

David Leeming writes of Polynesian, California Indian, African, and Mexican creation stories, along with an exploration of Egyptian cosmogony.[3] The stories told from within their own experiences speak of gods and spirits performing miraculous deeds from which life in all its forms emerges. The setting for the stories is a realm of spirit beings beyond the experience

---

2. Lebacqz and Driskill, *Ethics and Spiritual Care*, 23.
3. Leeming, *Voyage of the Hero*, 334–43.

and understanding of people. What the hearers do hear is that their life has its roots in beyondness. The gods have visited, and decided to form the earth and all its contents. Individual stories are contained in what he calls the "monomyth," expressing "our own journey through physical and psychic life, and of the evolutionary path of humanity to full consciousness."[4] Leeming's work is broken up into segments such as "Miraculous Conception" (pp. 9–50) and "Resurrection and Rebirth" (pp. 277–305), in each of which we can discern commonality in stories over a wide range of cultures and peoples. The particular matters that concern this book are found in the segment "Myths of Creation" (pp. 334–43). All the stories are clear. Always creation is the work of the gods, and beginnings are shrouded in mystery. Experience of mystery leads to questions of meaning. This in time engenders belief, and rituals to portray that belief.

Maria Harris, in *Proclaim Jubilee*, her exploration of Sabbath, makes explicit connections with both Jewish and Christian ritual and belief, and writes of the "healing, shimmering presence of God." She adds:

> Indeed Biblical religion, Jewish and Christian, conceives of spirituality—and its embodiment in prayer and in community and in ministry—as the exercise of the presence of God. This presence is awesome, thunderous, boring, occasionally ecstatic, regularly experienced as completely silent and full of mystery.[5]

One of the definitions applied to the word "exercise" is the performance of a function. If demonstrating the presence of God can be construed as a function, how then might this be contained in spirituality? The presence of God cannot be demonstrated, I believe, apart from the life and belief of those who claim a relationship with the divine. The believer's function is to live as if . . . ! This will be made more clear as the chapters unfold. It is clear, however, that relationship figures largely in all religious attachments. These attachments are not only to people but also to habitat and culture. Muriel Porter, in her book *Land of the Spirit*, encloses a paragraph about the strong religious attachments in Australian aboriginal spirituality:

> In Aboriginal spirituality, the creation of the world began in the Dreaming. Before the Dreaming there was a pre-existent formless substance, in which spirit beings lived. In some of the stories of the creation event, the Rainbow Serpent emerged from her long sleep underground when she realized her time to give birth had

---

4. Ibid., 6.
5. Harris, *Proclaim Jubilee*, 29.

Part Three: Spirituality—Recipe and Ingredients

come. She set free the spirit beings to create hills and valleys. . . . So, Australia . . . was born. The Serpent also set free the spirit beings to create animals and the human beings. . . . The snake . . . is regarded as the mother of the earth, the mother of all, and the spirit of the land.[6]

Scientifically, life emerged in basic forms evolving over millennia into more and more complex forms. People eventually emerged as the most complex of all. This development of people over millennia is a claim on mystery, and the myths of beginnings run parallel to, and complement, scientific theory. The myths and mysteries are themselves links to that we may term as "sacred." Wright and Sayre-Adams, cognisant of myth and mystery, define *sacred* as follows:

> The word *sacred* has its origins in the Latin *sacrare*: to consecrate or make holy. It is deeply imbued with religious and spiritual connotations, concerning rituals and practice associated with our desire to understand and connect with the divine such as sacred music or writings. The Bible, Qur'an and the Upanishads are sacred texts. Much of the finest music, prose and poetry across the generations has been inspired by and has sought to represent the sacred.[7]

My starting point is in the beginning myths of the Hebrew scriptures. In the early Biblical narrative, Genesis commences with "the earth was a formless void," a motif that is found in other beginning stories. The *Dictionary of Biblical Imagery* depicts it in this way:

> This motif takes its place in an ancient context of rival creation myths that centred on the ordering of chaos. Mesopotamian, Egyptian, and even Vedic Indian mythologies all talk about a chaos that is hostile to the creator god. In each case the creator god beats back the chaos to provide order, though chaos always remains a threat. The Bible's creation story is partly similar, inasmuch as God brings order out of chaos, but the biblical account is totally free of any threat or hostility in the chaos that God molds.[8]

While spirituality and creation have common features, and while the question of which came first may be asked, in the answering we may claim they both evolved out of chaos into order, and are still evolving, together having a constant impact on the life of people. Spirituality, as a human

6. Porter, *Land of the Spirit*, x.
7. Wright and Sayre-Adams, *Sacred Space*, 10–11.
8. Ryken et al., *Dictionary of Biblical Imagery*, 180.

experience, is founded on a perception of transcendence. The history of humanity suggests that this has always been the case. The presence of spirits is a most ancient element in the lives of people, and has influenced those lives in a host of ways. In every generation and culture this influence has differed. Ninian Smart informs us that "There is ample evidence that religious rites were practiced in early prehistoric times and it may be that the sense of the sacred has been part of man's experience from the very beginning." He continues: "It is notable that before the emergence of the human species proper (homo sapiens), Neanderthal Man—some one hundred and fifty thousand years ago—practiced the ritual interment of the dead. This seems to point to a belief in an afterlife of some kind, and to belief in an 'invisible' world."[9]

An individual's or group's experience of spirituality may be found encased in myths and dreams. Leeming, for example, writes:

> Most of us have had dreams of falling from a great height, of being lost, left behind, dreams of conquest.... Nearly every society has myths that express these themes on the group level.... on a deeper level their source is the universal soul of the human race itself.... The myths of the Aztecs reflect the particular reality of Mexico ... but when seen in conjunction with the myths of Iceland or Egypt or Greece, the Aztec myths reveal concerns which are common to all of us as a species.[10]

This commonality of concerns and understandings reflects a commonality in experiences of spirituality. This is on a deeper level than the particular religious attachments that are visible in any particular group.

Our lives are contained within the matrix of continuously evolving creation and an evolving spiritual presence. Nevertheless, as the evolving earth is not recognized as such by most of its inhabitants, so also spirituality evolving as a way of living is not recognized or understood by many. This is explicable if creation and spirituality are only understood as entities that can be recognized and held objectively. Tacey's claim of falling into spirituality, however, provides, if adequately considered, a different way of understanding: "To fall into spirituality is to fall into a larger pattern of reality, over which we have no control, and before which we stand astonished,

---

9. Smart, *Religious Experience of Mankind*, 33.
10. Leeming, *Voyage of the Hero*, 4.

Part Three: Spirituality—Recipe and Ingredients

mystified, and often disoriented. However, we do not fall into nothingness or emptiness; we fall into relationship with a secret or invisible other."[11]

Awareness of a larger pattern of reality, of deeper regions in life, can lead one to the edges of living, beyond which may be glimpsed a hint of chaos. Falling into relationship with an invisible other makes options previously unknown, visible.

Falling into such relationship is to begin to understand good and evil and thus be drawn into life patterns that will seek justice. There is an *is-ness* in both creation and spirituality. Creation continues and we have no choice but to be part of it, entering into the changes with hope. Along with creation, spirituality contains a core of relationship between human and holy. Recognition of creation requires a perception of change. Recognition of spirituality requires a perception of what might lie below the surface of our life. David Tacey contends that "the recognition of spirit has huge impacts on our mental and physical health, on our relationships, personal identity and work relations." It therefore "becomes vitally important that spirit is not held hostage by belief, prejudice, or ideology. Spirit has to be neutralized and brought into human reality, making it an essential aspect of human experience."[12]

The recognition of spirit runs the risk of being subverted when placed in the context of differing beliefs and religious standpoints. Arguments over the relative value of spiritual understandings will occur even among Christian denominations, let alone between faiths. There is a clear need to differentiate between the object and the perception of that object. If it is true that spirit and spirituality have links to the sacred, then perceptions of the sacred need to be acknowledged. Whether there be lots of gods or one, to claim attention to sacredness speaks of spirit. Spirit is not a particular being but a description of all that may take the title *god*. Spirituality is a way of life, and in its living can only be experienced in the common life of humanity, in which justice and mercy may be recognized.

Ingredients

In all this we will recognize a recipe for the understanding of spirituality. We need now to consider the ingredients that will allow the recipe to take shape and gain flavour. When we talk about ingredients, frequently

11. Tacey, *Spirituality Revolution*, 143.
12. Ibid., 201.

Part Three: Spirituality—Recipe and Ingredients

the business of baking a cake comes to mind. I guess all are aware that in the making of a cake ingredients are combined in specific ways and cooked with the object of obtaining a result—a cake that can be eaten and enjoyed. The ingredients in spirituality do not combine in the same way, nor can it be said through their processing, "I have spirituality." Ultimately, however, the end product is not the point. The point lies in the ingredients and the way in which they are enfolded into our lives. What can be said as we engage with the ingredients is that the spirit is visible in this or that person. At that point, as Tacey says, we have fallen into spirituality.

In the next chapters, therefore, a number of these ingredients are examined to enhance and give flavour and meaning to the recipe. As with all recipes, ingredients are listed. The list is attached. The amounts depend somewhat on the measure of intent in seeking to demonstrate spirituality.

3.1 Imaging the Divine

3.2 Hope

3.3 Awe

3.4 Music/Painting

3.5 Imagination

3.6 Seeing into the Depths

3.7 Darkness Covered the Earth

3.8 Justice

Meanings that we might attach to spirituality are of considerable importance in any exploration of spiritual care, to be considered as a way of life in which we may find expressions in elements of life experience. Life experience is linked to spirituality in ways that require exploration and eventual understanding. Each one of these ingredients is an aspect of spirituality, and of themselves, or in concert, they provide a description of its nature.

3.1. Imaging the Divine

The Biblical book of Genesis is the stuff of legends, and the very early chapters of Genesis are a harking back to the Jews' perceived beginnings, from a position of ongoing relationship with their God. The words, "Then God said, 'Let us make humankind in our own image, according to our likeness'" (Gen 1:26), reflect understandings from the very early history of the Israelite people. The beginnings of the nation lie in the wanderings of Abraham—part history, part legend. In those very early days there was no nation; rather, there were groups worshipping their own gods in company with other groups. Von Rad writes of these: "We have, of course, to assume that the groups worshipping respectively the God of Abraham, the Fear of Isaac, and the Strong One of Jacob, were originally distinct from one another."[1]

Von Rad writes of the origins of the Israelites and their arrival in Canaan as a number of loosely connected tribes or clans.[2] The clan league then founded at Shechem had no direct political functions. It was a sacral community, that is, it united the clans in the worship of the God Jahweh and the care of the common sanctuary."[3] "Bethel continued to attract large groups of worshippers. A god Bethel was worshipped there. Worship was offered to a god at Tabor, a local fertility and weather deity."[4] "Worship was also offered to a "Baal of the Covenant" (Judges 9:4) and at Beersheba to an El Olam (Genesis 22:33) and similarly, in the extreme south, to an El Roi."[5]

The creation story, as we well know, portrays God as creator. This image comes from within the lives of the Israelites as they travelled through the wilderness, and eventually into Canaan. It would have been one of their

1. Von Rad, *Old Testament Theology*, 7–8.
2 Ibid., 3–14.
3 Ibid., 17.
4 Ibid., 21.
5 Ibid., 22.

3.1. Imaging the Divine

legends, a story told around the campfire and in their tents. They recognized their lives as coming from the God of Abraham, the *I Am* who rescued them from Egypt and promised them a future. It comes from a time of settling down into a new land, and a beginning sense of nationhood.

There are many references in the Hebrew scriptures that suggest earlier beliefs in a variety of sacred figures. Such beliefs are in company with a plurality of belief in many cultures. Even at the time of its writing, beliefs in a multiplicity of gods was commonplace. This fits comfortably with the times, expressing common understandings. The oneness or uniqueness of God is a later phenomenon. The fact is, however, that in every religious form images have been drawn to depict the sacred, and to illustrate its relationship with human beings. The strength of this interaction between gods and people depends on perceptions of image, and this is recognized as differing across faith stances. The stance most visible and accessible to me is that portrayed through Jewish and Christian scriptures, and it is from this framework that much of the following is written.

Any idea of the nature of God can only be expressed in belief terminology. Such beliefs have no concrete bearing on the existence or otherwise of God. God cannot be demonstrated; belief can. The question therefore that emerges out of the statement "being made in the image of God" can only be answered in the context of belief. Much has been written, but ultimately the wide disparity of speculation on this question leaves us to conclude that the answer is still only mystery. Mark Edwards, researching the difficulties with this image, makes the point that:

> Enigma succeeds enigma when we are told that the man in the image of God was created male and female. Greek and English renderings imply a collective rather than an individual subject, but according to an early rabbinic construction of this verse the first created human was a hermaphrodite. This, one might maintain, was a necessity, since no being of either sex could possess the image of a Creator who has none.[6]

No doubt the enigma will remain and continue to intrigue scholars.

Garrett Green seeks to discover links between theology and religious imagination. He writes of a different way of considering the image of God (*imago Dei*), traditionally claimed as located in the soul. Green is more interested in relationship, and makes the following statement:

---

6. Edwards, *Image*, 9.

> Interpreting the *imago* relationally avoids the long-disputed issue of its content. Whatever its "nature" may be, the text is telling us, the *imago* represents the original *relationship* between divine and human: man is *like* God in some basic and definitive way. There is a "family resemblance" between God and human beings. It would be only a slight exaggeration to say that according to Genesis the content of the image is the relationship it posits between God and man.[7]

To speak of being made in the image of God is to speak of an unsolvable mystery. It requires in the first instance a description of God, and this is never forthcoming. The Hebrew scriptures are clear that no one can see God. Imaging God therefore may be considered visible in the quality of relationship. Relationships between people vary greatly, so if it is to be an image of God, God must therefore be considered in particular ways that can be recognized as good. From the Hebrew scriptures we glean a number of qualities of God. In the first place, God is creator, and recognizes the creation as good. Secondly, God rescues the people from slavery because he loves them, not because they were particularly worthy.

Pictures are painted throughout the scriptures, and in the pictures we can recognize descriptions of relationship. Some of these pictures we find in the biblical Deuteronomy:

> For you are a people holy to the LORD. . . . It was not because you were more numerous. . . . It was because the LORD loved you and kept the oath that he swore to your ancestors . . . redeemed you from the house of slavery. . . . Know therefore that the LORD your God is . . . the faithful God who maintains covenant loyalty with those who love him . . . (Deut 7:6–9)

Key words that point us to relationship include: loved, kept his promise, redeemed, faithful, maintains covenant.

In the Hebrew scriptures God is never identified in any concrete form. Frequently there are dreams and visions. God passes by in the wind; God appears as fire. Moses cannot look at God, but his face was allowed to shine for the people as a reflection of God's glory. God is heard as the voice of silence, but also recognized in fire and brimstone. God calls, anoints, sets aside, judges, and reconciles, but always through intermediaries. God is distanced from, but also intimately involved in, the life of *his* people. Acts of God, and the very nature of God, is interpreted by people with all their

---

7. Green, *Imagining God*, 86–87.

frailties of understanding. God sends angels as messengers but stays away *himself*. This was the Jewish experience of God as far as we can ascertain. Certainly the holiness of God was not a matter for debate. It was true and final.

I want to claim two life elements as settings for expounding the image of God. These are relationship and creation. In our day, creation is not considered a one-off event with a beginning and an end, but a setting in place of a continuous process. The geological history of the earth is a cogent reminder of the changes that occur daily in the formation of the earth. Relationship and creation are clearly part of each other, and together proclaim a viable example of an image of the sacred in the lives of people. They do not of themselves depict an image of a sacred entity, but to the discerning onlooker demonstrate a way of life that differs from the commonplace. Thus, loving, keeping promises, being faithful, maintaining agreements—in short, being truthful and living with integrity—become the badges of life lived within a spiritual framework. Each of these descriptors also enables creativity, opening pathways along which others may travel as authentic human beings.

That travel will also honour and protect the earth, if not for the sake of sharing the creative process, for the sake of peace and life. Earth pathways that allow us to travel authentically will clearly not be destructive in any way. Creativity is not only about birthing something new, it is also about preserving integrity in day-to-day activity. There is no place for war in this process. War only destroys. It has no productive potential. Destruction of life, destruction of habitat, may be considered the shadow side of creation. Even a small-scale war has a vast impact on the life of the earth. Consistently we forget the picture of a blue sphere hanging in space. Any action that destroys a portion of this blue sphere may be considered an act of violence, for it impacts all.

Creation is an ongoing process. One immediate understanding of the process is necessarily focused on the earth. It is where we live. It is what provides meaning and substance for life. We cannot live without it. While we read in the Bible that God created the earth, we cannot read into it the notion that this was a specific one-off event, occurring in the distant past, and happening under the hand of a divine being during a given amount of time. What we do know is that a process of change continues. This is subject to forces contained in the earth, and subject to weather patterns in which we find fire and flood. Earthquakes and other volcanic activity are constant reminders that the earth is not as stable as once was considered. Creation and re-creation continue.

The presence of life is intimately linked to the life of the earth, and indeed is part of the creative changes that occur. Evidence for change, and the rise and fall of life forms, is all around us, and is given shape and form through the work of archeologists, biologists, and geographers. Specialized investigation has revealed vast changes in the shape of the earth and the shape of life. We are part of this evolutionary process, with our own ancestors reaching back though time. One important factor in the progression is relationship. From earliest times it is clear that people gathered in groups. Clans and families provided the glue that held people together, and allowed them to discover and develop new and different fields of understanding.

Relationship, like creation, is a continuous process. Relationship requires engagement, not just once but continuously. The quality of a relationship is observable in mutual dealings, connectedness, and feeling. These may be discerned in the links between people, but may also be visible in the ways in which nations interact. We might say that both individuals and nations may image the divine in the quality of their interactions. This is also particularly important for the world's life and health.

In our world the relationship between countries of like history and like language is gauged satisfactory if, in the political and cultural maneuvering of the nations, there is nevertheless mutual understanding and belonging. What is more problematic, and therefore more important for the world, are the relationships between differing countries. A much greater commitment to maintenance of relationship is needed.

Recognizing the varieties in relationship that exist in the world, it also becomes important that we recognize variety in religious values and practices and with those, the varieties of understanding of the nature of the divine. This means facing the reality that ideas of God as one, along with meanings attached to image, are theological renderings about something we cannot know, but which appeal to us, and are rooted in the religious life of Jews, from whom Christianity sprang. This in turn leads us back to the earlier statement about being made in the image of God. If this is only linked to the notion of potential holiness, it becomes in our time unsustainable. If it is only linked to the Christian way, I suggest this also is unsustainable. The message of the Hebrew scriptures is of a wholly other God who chooses to engage with people in a covenant relationship that requires the people to respond with belief and loyalty. The image is displayed in life

3.1. Imaging the Divine

through ritual and rule. Being made in the image therefore is a goal, only fulfilled in some eternal abode. What appears as more important was their unshakable belief that they were God's chosen.[8]

As God's chosen, they could never be ultimately neglected by God, even though they had to endure wars and exile at a national level, and a plethora of rules that left many as outcasts, some literally banned from the community. With all this in mind, the church grasped the stories of Jesus and made of them a visitation, and a sacrifice by God to re-establish the image. This Jesus is now, in the eyes of the church, the Son of God, and the one to whom reverence and worship is due as he shares a place with God in heaven, and claims the lives of believers in a relationship that is said to be of love. A fundamental problem of the image of God still remains, exacerbated in some ways by the insistence of the church on a Trinitarian belief standpoint.

Christianity, Judaism, and Islam, in claiming the oneness of God, project a sense of superiority over those whose religious tradition appears to associate life with many emanations of god. Christianity has taken this a step further with its claims of Jesus' Sonship, and therefore of God's enhanced relationship with those who believe. Jesus, as the Son of God who shows though his life and death the true nature of God, is, in the mind of the church, the definitive image of God.

I wonder, however, whether in spiritualizing the life of Jesus we don't take him out of his human context, and place him in a position that is beyond our understanding and control. The claims of the Gospels, stories of Jesus in the church, place his life in a series of miraculous events, particularly healings. His words are not ordinary sayings, but are always linked to spiritual sources. I think we need to ask, what is it that Jesus did as a man among his people, the Jews?

A story in John's Gospel (8:1–11) tells us a great deal. The laws were very harsh, particularly against women. A woman suspected of adultery should be stoned to death—a horrific and cruel punishment. In this, the twenty-first century, women are still stoned to death for the same reason, or for lesser *crimes*, frequently by their own families to assuage *their shame*.

In our story, a woman was dragged before Jesus and thrown on the ground at his feet. Claiming to have caught her in the act, the men demanded that the law be upheld—that Jesus acquiesce in the punishment they planned to carry out. The law was the law, but Jesus attaches a condition:

8. Ibid.

"Let anyone among you who is without sin be the first to throw a stone at her" (8:7). One by one they went away. Amongst the harshness of the law, the cruelty of those planning to carry it out, and the raw fear and hopelessness of the woman, we find in Jesus' response compassion, forgiveness, justice, sensibility to feelings, non-judgementalism, and ultimately freedom for the woman.

On another occasion John the Baptist, in prison, was concerned to know whether the Messiah, whose coming he had proclaimed along with dreams of freedom from the oppression of Rome, had finally come in the person of Jesus. The response was provided, not as John expected, but in terms of what was happening: "He answered them, Go and tell John what you have seen and heard: the blind receive their sight, the lame walk, the lepers are cleansed, the deaf hear, the dead are raised, the poor have good news brought to them" (Luke 7:21–23).

These two stories give body to a radical change occurring among the Jews of Jesus' day. They are not windows into messiahship. They portray an incursion into the regulated life of the people, a new way of looking at life. In this way Jesus' actions were prophetic. Difference was present. Difference could be grasped and life expectations changed. We could say that this was creation in progress, continuing in the lives of the people in the new possibilities being offered. Here the image of God becomes visible.

In our time this notion of God's image is really quite profound. It is concerned with the total life of people, and this includes relationship with each other, with the earth, and with that which is sacred. The image, to have effect in the world, must be all-inclusive; all people are affected, all people live on the earth, all people carry within the spirit of holiness.

In the Hebrew creation story God says, "It is all very good." All aspects are invested with honour. God is named as the creator of all things. The creator begins the future, considers all things good, invests all with honour, brings into existence, and has originality and imagination. It is in this process that humankind comes into being, and is invited to stay.

It can also be claimed that people enter into life essentially good, and that all people have the ability to imagine and produce original thinking and action. Matthew Fox, a number of years ago, published *Original Blessing*, in which he claims that a new paradigm of faith will not only be of supreme benefit to Christians, but will also open pathways for a recognition of other faiths. He says, in the context of his introduction to his book:

3.1. Imaging the Divine

> The creation-centred spiritual tradition is truly ecumenical. All persons and all religions share creation in common. A global awakening can only happen from a spiritual awakening that is of global dimensions. As we move from an *egological* to an *ecological* consciousness, this basic understanding of our true interdependence will overcome our tendencies to make battle with each other.[9]

These words—all persons and all religions share creation in common—are overshadowed at times by claims of political supremacy, religious superiority, and rights to heaven, each of which is at times forcefully supported. In company with claims for land and the subsequent changing of boundaries, populations are uprooted and forced to flee to places where they are not wanted. Life for them becomes hard and bitter. When claims to religious superiority are imposed on others with violence, there is a clear implication that those others have no right to a share in creation. When God is invoked to support the superiority claims, the image of God is deeply tarnished.

The likeness of God has nothing to do with look-alikes, or behavioral similarities, or of humans being superior to other animals. Rather, it is a matter of entering into creation with a desire to make things new. Making things new will necessitate a particular attitude to others, a specific response to the world's direction of travel. Leonard Swidler's conclusion to his work on the *Meaning of Life*, in which he says, "Although cultures remain distinct, they can no longer remain untouched by others. All of our different cultures must now live within a Global culture,"[10] is even more pertinent in the twenty-first century. Similar are his comments on religion:

> Several of the world religions and ideologies have attempted to dominate the world, and four of them have had rather remarkable success: Buddhism, Christianity, Islam, and Marxism. . . . it is clear from experience that no one of these, or any other, religion/ideology will be completely triumphant and destroy all the rest. . . . The religions of the world (also) must now live within a Global Dialogue.[11]

Global dialogue is an essential key in the deliverance of people from the excesses of change. Delivery and recovery for humanity will be hindered

---

9. Fox, *Original Blessing*, 15.
10. Swindler, *Meaning of Life*, 115.
11. Ibid., 115–16.

dramatically if we cannot entertain the realities of change. We bear the image of God when we enter into creativity, and creativity has dialogue for a running partner. Without this the image is shadowy, a reflection that we are not able to hold. Imaging the divine frequently fails on the world stage when the imaging only reflects our personal choices, beliefs, and needs. The image we project is most important, for always it is under the scrutiny of the world's people. All religions have problems with this, and all religions project images that are both good and bad. The image projecting is confusing to all, and when religious groups vie with each other over which image is more true, confusion is exacerbated.

Perhaps the most helpful image is one that aligns the divine with justice, responsibility, and integrity. These are the matters that smooth the path towards peace and equality. These are the images that will lead to change and the recognition that all have value. These are the images that, speaking to creativity, assist people to be whole, and wholesome in their living with each other, and with their God. Entering into creativity is an entering into hope in which all is good. The creation story contains robust actions that demand attention. It is not about a choice to arrive or not. The wind of God blows, and touches all and sundry with life. Life is not defined as nice or not nice. It just is! The good is in its *isness*.

Spirituality, therefore, portraying the image of that which is holy, contains in its portrayal an acknowledgement that life, consisting of many things, contains the essential element of sacredness, informing the way we live, and the attitude we portray in everyday interactions.

3.2. Hope

JULIAN OF NORWICH (C. 1343–1417) writes of one of the revelations she received that Jesus said to her, "It behoved that there should be sin; but all shall be well, and all shall be well, and all manner of thing shall be well."[1] In Christianity, as in many other religious forms, hope has a particular shape which appears at times attached to visions of an afterlife, and personal and visible life with God. For some it also includes a meeting with old friends and loved ones. This hope, however, is frequently considered as containing a caveat about sin, written in as it were to the rites of passage.

The Christian church has through the centuries majored in sin, so much so that even today, in virtually every expression of church, forgiveness for sin is sought every time there is a gathering for worship. One version of the baptismal service in one of the churches contains these words: "The word of God teaches that we are born sinful and unclean, but God washes us clean in the waters of baptism, and we are born again as his children." In another worship book, baptismal candidates or the parents of babies are asked, "Do you repent of your sins?" Prayers of confession frequently begin, "Let us confess our sins to God."

Hope is frequently expressed as forgiveness that redirects one's steps towards the ultimate goal of life: being in heaven, face to face with God. Such a hope also contains an expectation of the renewal of relationships previously experienced in this earthly life, and severed through death. Hope at times also considers that, provided one's faith is strong, illness, wrongness, and all that debilitates life will be in some way rectified and life restored. The expectation of hope is that God will be on our side, and provide all that is necessary for us to continue our life. Those who have recovered well from

---

1. Julian of Norwich, *Revelations of Divine Love*, ch. 27.

whatever beset them frequently lay claim to the goodness of God. This of course raises the serious question of God's goodness for those who do not survive, or whose lives are cut short by disease, war, and so on.

The *Oxford Dictionary of English* defines hope as "a feeling of expectation and desire for a particular thing to happen," along with confidence in the possibility of its fulfillment.[2] This is, to a considerable extent, the way in which hope is understood in the church. When hope is located primarily in our thinking, however, it runs the risk of changing to hopelessness when things do not turn out as we anticipate. Hope such as this asks the question "why me?" when life takes a turn for the worse. Hoping that one's life can be acceptable to God, and that faith in Jesus is a pathway into heaven, has also over time led to a denigration of the earth.

Shoring up one's religious viewpoint, whether taking revenge, planning to ensure the emergence of conservative government, extending the visibility of one's own church, or engaging in political brinkmanship, does not engender hope. The notion of hope for the world does not seem to be, in current world politics, something that the world's religions hold in high regard. The world, however, will not find direction in life if religions simply present their own viewpoints about the God they consider to be their own. People do not need to be told that this or that God is true, and will be found when connection is made with this or that viewpoint.

A heaven-and-earth dichotomy has left the earth in the place of a rather poor second. We are now reaping the result of this as, through our destructive ways, the earth has begun to warm beyond what is acceptable for adequate life. Destruction of forests, ejecting smoke and soot into the air, and the rapid and almost unsustainable growth in the number of inhabitants are in part a result of overreliance on current life as the fulfillment of all that is necessary for our enjoyment. There does not appear to be any place or time in which to step back and review our actions, and consider appropriate ways to renew our approach to life.

There was clearly, in the early times of the Israelites, a recognition of the importance of reflection and renewal. The Hebrew scriptures established, among the rules of their life, space and time for review and renewal. This time was known as Jubilee.

> You shall hallow the fiftieth year and you shall proclaim liberty throughout the land to all its inhabitants. It shall be a jubilee for you: you shall return, every one of you, to your property and every

---

2. Stevenson, ed., *Oxford Dictionary of English*, 844.

one of you to your family. That fiftieth year shall be a jubilee for you: you shall not sow, or reap the after growth, or harvest the unpruned vines. For it is a jubilee; it shall be holy to you: you shall eat only what the field itself produces. (Lev 25:10–12)

This may well be an impossible task in the twenty-first century, but it does express an important truth for us all about the value and importance of review time, both personally and for the earth—a time for the renewal of hope.

Maria Harris writes of Jubilee, reminding us of this ancient Jewish ideal of renewal and freedom every fifty years. She reminds us also of the many times we have jubilees of relationship in modern times.

> Jubilee's ancient meaning, however, remains the genesis and the foundation for this better-known and more popular understanding, even when celebrants are unaware of it. Etymologically, Jubilee's meaning may come from the Hebrew verb *ybl*, which signifies release especially from debt, although it is far more usual to find experts citing *yobel* as the foundation of the word. *Yobel* is the Hebrew term for a ram's horn or trumpet sounded in a public arena. That reverberating trumpet heralds celebration, music, and song.[3]

In such celebration we may discern hope.

Questions that assail us in our days ask: where lies hope in the midst of drought and flood; where lies hope in the cruelty and fanaticism of fundamentalism; where lies hope in abject poverty; where lies hope in refugees returned to danger; where lies hope in the midst of war? None of these have a simple answer, and religious platitudes are of no value. Answers are complex, and at times appear impossible to find.

Almost daily in news broadcasts and newspapers we are told of people hoping for a solution to a traumatic happening in their lives. Many hope against hope that matters will turn out well. But when hopes are dashed, what then? So many of us pin our hopes on future events or possibilities. Hope, however, is terrible if it is only in our mind. Hope becomes futile when the things we had hoped for do not eventuate. It is then that we cry out for answers, and despair when they are unsatisfactory. Hope is always linked to possibilities of sadness and loss, but if sadness and loss displace hope, then truly life will become dire.

The word "hope" has a nice sound, and for many is found in a quiet religious belief that looks beyond this life to life hereafter. But this is simply

---

3. Harris, *Proclaim Jubilee*, 96.

not the lot of millions of people throughout the world. For the people of the world to catch a glimpse of hope, it is necessary that individuals, groups, communities, and nations begin to speak to each other of things to be done to turn the life of the world around. It requires some to share with others their desire for peace and justice, along with possible strategies that will allow it to happen. It requires all to learn a different language—that of love and compassion. It requires all to give a little in order that all might share. It requires a hard look at the earth as alive and hurting, along with a commitment to begin to heal it.

Hope is not a fun word but one that confronts us with our lack of hope, and the risk of world catastrophe, and compels us to look again at life and our part in it. In *Tales of a Magic Monastery* we read:

> I thought it good fortune to go to the Magic Monastery for Christmas. But at the foot of the hill sat a blind beggar, and when I drew near to give him some money, I heard him ask, "Who will lead me into the heart of God?" I couldn't go on. Who would lead him into the heart of God? I sat down in front of him. I took his hands. "Together," I said. "Together we'll go into the heart of God."[4]

The story as written stands alone. But I think all such stories invite us to enter more deeply. I wonder what the beggar meant by his question, and I guess part of the answer may be found in the assumption that the *heart of God* was very important. So we might ask, what does it mean to go into the heart of God, and how is this linked to hope? Lots of questions tumble over each other; some are answered according to one's religious affiliation. A beating heart, of course, signifies life. When we listen to our own heart, we become aware of our own life, but also of the possibility that it might stop. Hope holds fast to the beat, and gets on with making life count. Life, as we all know, is evident in a multitude of forms, some of which are destructive, others a result of ill health and circumstance.

To go into the heart of God is a journey in the company of hope. It is not, however, a matter of me hoping that it will be great when I arrive. Rather, it is the kind of hope that sustains the journey and values all the experiences—good and bad. The reality for us all is that life is happening right now. Good or bad, life takes us along the journey. When hope travels with us, that journey is full of happenings that fill out our years. I visited a friend after many years of being away. His heart was erratic, he was overweight,

---

4. Theophane the Monk, *Tales of a Magic Monastery*, 54.

3.2. HOPE

he was incontinent, and the evidence of all this was pervasive. But he grew beautiful cacti.

Going into the heart of God, consciously journeying towards the sacred, will not benefit us if we neglect our surroundings on the way. In the world religions, going into the heart of God is a journey into total peace and contentment. This brief story suggests that travelling companions may be needed, and that the travelling may be more important than the goal. Is it possible, for example, that in taking the hand of the beggar that which is divine for us may be discerned?

Hope set in the future has no future if the present is neglected, and left to spoil on the vine. Hope needs to step out into space and look back at the jewel called earth, and then join with the earth and all its people to recognize its unity, and the artificiality of so much that we hold dear. Hope needs to be understood as a present reality, as a way of life in which is contained the understanding that life must be lived. In the living we will come to understand that all aspects of life are of value and should be valued as such. Hope must not be subverted by constant calls to seek forgiveness for sin, whether in the present or as a result of some mythical event in the distant past.

Lived hope, as distinct from a projection into the future, contains the elements of confidence and courage. Life contains a host of variations, and in those we find both good and bad experiences. Confidence will take hold of the good as a reinforcement for life and a motivation for maintaining relationships with others. Confidence allows us to make decisions with courage, and to undertake the task of creatively living in the world. Creative living understands the realities of life, and considers them with a clear and open eye. Hopeful living, however, is not super-optimistic, nor does it become a fantasy ride. Hopeful living recognizes the bad as potentially destructive, but also as a possible stepping stone to better things. A hopeful life does not simply bemoan the injustice of becoming ill or loosing something precious, but seeks way of acting and living justly and compassionately. A hopeful life finds ways to cut through the weeds in order to find fertile soil. Hopeful living also pursues the inward journey, wherein we find strength, interdependence, and creativity, living life-changing moments. It means engaging in change, taking time to reflect, and allowing stillness and movement to follow one another.

The tradition that encompasses the Christian hope is firmly set on renewed life with God after death, and a promise, affirmed in the church,

Part Three: Spirituality—Recipe and Ingredients

of fellowship with the risen and ascended Jesus. Hebblethwaite reminds us, however, that this has not always been the case. He says:

> For the most part, in ancient Israel's belief, the breath of life is God's own spirit animating a human being, and when that human being dies this spirit "returns to God who gave it" (Eccles. 12:7). It is quite mistaken to take that as referring to the immortality of the soul. Rather, it is God's spirit that returns to God.[5]

Hope will not be engendered by pious words, nor necessarily by a faith viewpoint. Rather, it will be more likely visible in the compassion and love of others who remain with those most affected.

A sense of presence becomes tangible when people of all faiths, and of none, remember their humanity and reach out from within their life to those in need. In that shared reaching out the spirit may be felt, for each brings his or her own relationship with the spirit of the holy. Martyn Percy questions whether we may assume the church to be offering "a capacious and transitional space for encounters with God, a place enabling both transformation and dwelling and for confronting the suffering and joy of human life".[6] It may be true that the church offers such a canopy, but this has more meaning for those whose faith has a Christian flavour, even though some in the wider church may have doubts. I think we can speak more meaningfully of a spiritual canopy under which all people may encounter the holy.

Such a canopy with so broad a spread may be considered by some to be too thin to embrace the whole of humankind. Those who have a fundamentalist position within their faith may be prone to this consideration. If, however, we move beyond *ecclesial canopies*, we enter the realm of ambiguity, in which the claim of faith in God must consider the faith of those in some other faith. We cannot deny the possibility—indeed the probability—of a spiritual canopy under which people may find hope and faith for their lives, and confidence in the future.

Confidence will take hold of the bad, being prepared for consequences, but also finding ways to guide one's life through the impact of difficulties. Bad experiences may happen through our own actions, or through the actions of others, or even because we happen to be in a wrong place at the wrong time. Confidence will enable us to take a responsible position in our

---

5. Hebblethwaite, *Christian Hope*, 15.
6. Percy, *Ecclesial Canopy*, 183.

responses. All experiences contain possibilities for life changes, and hopeful living will recognize, and take hold of, and make use of such possibilities.

John Makranski's chapter in *Hosting the Stranger* discusses the awakening of hospitality. He illustrates this through a story of his own experience as a stranger, and asks us who might be the stranger in our own life.

> On a daily basis, the strangers all around me don't automatically evoke from me the spontaneous loving concern that I feel for dear ones and intimate friends. Unless the stranger provides a specific reason, unless he justifies his worth to me in some specific way, I do not spontaneously esteem or appreciate him. . . . Buddhist philosophers have argued that this feeling of apathy to strangers is common to human beings and subconsciously conditions all our social interactions and social disclosures.[7]

It is obvious that all are strangers to someone else, so the question may well be how strangers will provide and receive hospitality. This chapter speaks to hope, and it occurs to me that hope and hospitality belong together. When strangers remain strangers there is a possibility that hospitality will fail, and that along with this hope will diminish. I don't think one can be hospitable if one is fearful.

A classic biblical story about hospitality and hope comes to us from the book of Genesis. The hero is Abraham.

> The LORD appeared to Abraham by the oaks of Mamre, as he sat at the entrance of his tent in the heat of the day. He looked up and saw three men standing near him. When he saw them, he ran from the tent entrance to meet them, and bowed down to the ground. He said, "My lord, if I find favor with you, do not pass by your servant. Let a little water be brought, and wash your feet, and rest yourselves under the tree. Let me bring a little bread, that you may refresh yourselves, and after that you may pass on . . ." (Gen 18:1–5)

Much is being said about extremism and the possibility—even likelihood—of terrorism. The stranger is viewed with suspicion. When we become mired in the fallout from extreme terrorist actions elsewhere, the resulting feelings of fear undermine hopeful living. Fear shuts our life down. We shut doors and turn keys as we attempt to thwart any possibilities for extremism in our place. At the same time, suspicion emerges and blaming begins. Hopeful living acknowledges all these possibilities, even their

---

7. Macranski, "Awakening of Hospitality," 107.

reality, but still considers life to contain creativity, and companionship, and trust. There will always be strangers in our life. We cannot know everybody, nor be even familiar with them.

Hopeful living will recognize the stranger in myself, and therefore allow me to stop being a stranger and find instead ways of offering hospitality. Hopefulness leads to hospitality; there is a kindness in relationship that recognizes the humanity in others. Hope is a way of life, and is clearly linked in my mind to the hospitality of others, and a sense of connection with those who once had been strangers.

Hope now has the potential for awareness of worthwhileness. It contains the seeds of self-acceptance, and acceptance of others. It enables the recognition of social values and cohesion. It shows that we belong. These together allow for the glass to be half full. It helps us to hold that, whatever we find in life, the outcome will be acceptable. It is a recognition that life is. Julian's claim is now located in the present, and in our daily living.

Thomas Moore writes, towards the end of *The Re-Enchantment of Everyday Life*, of practicalities that establish our lives and maintain some sort of balance. "Life may appear to be complete," he writes, with all these applications, but "what is missing in all this is the penetrating enchantment of every experience that rises out of a world that is alive and that has deep and mysterious roots of power."[8] In this hope resides, and all will be well!

---

8. Moore, *Re-Enchantment of Everyday Life*, 369.

3.3. Awe

Dictionaries define *awe* as "overwhelming wonder, respect, or dread; power to inspire fear or reverence."[1] Reading and pondering this definition leads to the question: in what way might life be awe filled? Little children are filled with awe in each new discovery they make. Much that adults consider ordinary is magical for children in the exploration of their life, the magical clearly evidenced in their facial expressions. Many things and many experiences make for feelings of awe.

Prophetic narratives in the biblical story of the faith life of the Israelites engendered for them a sense of wonder and reverence for their God. An example of these comes to us from the book of Isaiah:

> In the year that King Uzziah died, I saw the Lord sitting on a throne high and lofty; and the hem of his robe filled the temple. Seraphs were in attendance above him; each had six wings: with two they covered their faces, and with two they covered their feet, and with two they flew. And one called to another and said: "Holy, holy, holy is the LORD of Hosts; the whole earth is full of his glory." The pivots on the thresholds shook at the voices of those who called, and the house was filled with smoke. And I said, "Woe is me! I am lost, for I am a man of unclean lips, and I live among a people of unclean lips; yet my eyes have seen the King, the LORD of hosts!" (Isa 6:1–5)

In Mark's Gospel, coming from the life of early Christian communities, there is a story in which the disciples are in a boat on a very stormy lake, in fear of their lives and angry with Jesus, who was fast asleep. Eventually, however, he woke up and, taking in the situation, "said to the sea,

---

1. Little et al., *Shorter Oxford English Dictionary*, 140.

'Peace! Be still!' Then the wind ceased, and there was a dead calm. He said to them, "Why are you afraid? Have you still no faith?" And they were filled with great awe and said to one another, "Who then is this, that even the wind and sea obey him?" (4:39–41).

From these biblical stories, we might claim that those who experienced the events depicted in the narratives found in them a sense of sacred presence. The many stories in the biblical narrative are more than mythology. They engage real people who, even if their experiences were more a dream than physical reality, were left with a sense of wonderment and dread. Sacred space, however, is not something only found in history or mythology. Space becomes sacred as people experience something of spiritual presence. This may happen in walking a labyrinth, or entering a cave, or standing on the edge of a cliff with the sea below, or on top of a mountain, in company or alone, or indeed in any other space encountered in life's journeying.

The point of all biblical stories was to engender a sense of wonder, and inspire reverence for God. As such, they almost certainly had the desired effect in their time. We, being far more prosaic, look on them as interesting, but having limited application in this modern world. They don't generally inspire us with awe. This does not, however, inhibit the possibility of being awestruck by other's stories, or our own stories and visions.

Awe, of course, is not only attached to stories and visions. It is found in the discoveries of natural wonders—Uluru (commonly known as Ayre's Rock), the Grand Canyon, enormous breaking waves, the power unleashed in cyclonic winds, active volcanoes, and much more. It is found in the tiny creatures that inhabit the earth, and through the microscope even smaller forms of life. Much that impinges on our senses from the world around us leaves us awestruck. Some of this awe is attached to the recognition that the earth is not merely a lump of rock, but an organism that is alive, and active, and always in transition. Its activity and its changing form is something we cannot control, but we can adjust our life to live with the earth, not just on it. In treating the world with respect we will recognize it as an interconnected whole.

In the southwestern corner of Western Australia, near the place where two oceans meet, one can observe enormous waves that, when they break, overwhelm everything in their path. Even more gigantic waves have engulfed villages and towns in Indonesia and Japan in the last few years. They are all irresistible, devastating. They inspire dread, capable as they

3.3. Awe

are of crushing everything in their path. They are awe-full to behold. They provide evidence of forces far beyond our comprehension, and remind us continually of our ever-changing world. They remind us also that, despite all our efforts to manipulate the earth, there is much that is far beyond our control.

There are times when we are awed by the achievements of people despite all difficulties. Some of these may be within our personal experience; some we read about, and some are presented visually through our television and on the big theatre screen. In July 1969 the unthinkable happened. Almost a retelling of early science fiction stories featuring Buck Rogers and his space adventures, a man stepped out of a capsule on to the surface of the moon. That event, beamed back to earth and broadcast to the world on television sets, had millions sitting and watching, awestruck by the sight of a man on the moon.

A key element in all that inspires us with awe is relationship. Life takes place for each of us within a complex web of interactions. Unlike the spider's web, designed to entrap, the web that binds us together enhances our understanding of life. We are linked to all others in the world because of our humanity. Irrespective of religion, language, and culture, our fundamental connection is being human. All are born; all live; all die. We are each, however, born into a particular set of circumstances that frame and shape our life. Culture, religion, and language are part of our inheritance, and the common features of these life elements link us together as groups. All have a relationship with the land in which the culture flourishes, and land provides much of the sustenance needed for life. Groups became nations, and nations interact with each other on the borders. These have been established sometimes by force, sometimes by agreement, but all have the effect of containment for each of the groups.

Beyond these borders, however, we are all contained on the earth. We cannot move beyond its borders. We explore the space beyond those borders, but for now always with limitations and always in the knowledge that people who do travel into space must return or die. The earth is our island in the vastness of the universe. It is the one place on which life may be sustained. It is our home.

Home, as distinct from a house, is the place into which we are born, within which we develop our understanding of life, and from which we venture into the wider world to seek our fortune. For some this is a search for fame and wealth, for others a search for understanding and wisdom.

Part Three: Spirituality—Recipe and Ingredients

For all it is an extension of relationship, to encompass those who until now have been strangers. The core component in all the travels we undertake, whether each day, through the years, or over the vast distances of space on our island spaceship, is our relationship with ourselves. Wright and Sayre-Adams write of this journey as one in which

> The shift of consciousness that comes as we enter into right relationship with our deepest selves, our innermost being, utterly transforms our view of the world and our place in it. We "see through things," understanding better what is real and what is illusion, what is important and what is unimportant. Consciousness of the self has been the key to all sacred traditions, for it is in knowing the self that we go beyond the self, to that place or part of us, that state of being which down the ages has been called the divine, the absolute God.

They continue on to say that such knowing of oneself is paradoxical in that "This knowing of the self has often been suppressed down through the ages. It is too dangerous to established authority; far better to keep people in their place through rigid adherence to codes and dogmas, be they religious, political or organizational."[2]

Home frequently becomes a sacred space to which we refer, and sometimes regularly return. Recognition of a sacred space varies from individual to individual. In company it may be less possible to reach agreement. Recognition of sacredness, in which one is surprised or led to wonderment or reverence, is more likely an individual experience. Relationships also are experienced as sacred. Such experience contains the risk of being problematic if it is perceived to challenge familial or community interests, or in the context of links with a religious organization. If that organization has strongly established practices, conflict may occur. Some of these conflicts have been reported in the media. Some of these conflicts involving family and community have had fatal consequences. The experience of awe may become an experience of terror.

Children's encounters in the early years of life can result in times of awe, and of fear. In the life of a child, awe may be engendered from something very small, as well as things very large. Largeness is experienced differently depending on the size of the child at the time. I can distinctly remember, as a small child, while out for a walk with my mother, being confronted by two men on horseback. We lived in a small country town. At

---

2. Wright and Sayre-Adams, *Sacred Space*, 5.

3.3. Awe

that time local butchers prepared their own meat, beginning with the live bullock. On this particular day, a bullock had escaped from a holding yard, and the men were out looking for it. As we walked along, the men on their horses galloped up, stopped, and asked if we had seen their bullock. We had not seen it, so they galloped on.

What I saw were two very big men seated far above me on the backs of two very big unquiet horses that had been galloping around the streets. Their heaving breathing and staring eyes were most disquieting. It was for me an awe-full experience. I have remained cautious about horses since that day.

Awe, and its association with amazement, and surprise, and astonishment, is a short step away from terror, and needs therefore to also engage with reverence and veneration. For this to happen, for awe to turn away from terror, it is helpful to withdraw or turn aside into some place or space wherein we can take stock of amazement and integrate it carefully into our being. We are, after all, part of a whole, interconnected because of our humanity, and firmly related to each other as people.

Wright and Sayre-Adams write of labyrinths as pathways to the sacred. These can be constructed on a particular model and can be found in many places. One of these places that springs to mind is Grace Cathedral in San Francisco. They add, however:

> With a little imagination, it is possible to walk a labyrinthine route around the streets near our homes or places of work. . . . a large part of the impact is determined by our preparation, commitment and actions as we follow a particular path. The process is as important as the outcome. Many people, when troubled . . . instinctively take a walk. This purposeful walking is clearly related to the principle of walking the labyrinth.[3]

Awe touches the threads that tie us to spirit presence. We don't normally think about something that is awe-full; we experience the awe deep inside. It can awaken tears, feelings of reverence, and may even conjure up fear, but thinking doesn't occur until later, when we try to examine our experience. One result of this is a recognition that the place of the experience suggests a sacred space. The biblical story of Jacob wrestling with God is an example. In that narrative, "Jacob called the place Peniel, saying, 'For I have seen God face to face, and yet my life is preserved'" (Gen 32:30).

3. Ibid., 77.

Sacred space provides for solitude and silence, in which we can meditate on awe, and its place in our life with the spirit. It matters little how we name the spirit. It is important to be still and hear what name the spirit calls itself, and what name it addresses you by.

Thomas à Kempis was a Christian religious in the fifteenth century, well known for the production of a series of meditations under the title *The Imitation of Christ*. Whatever our faith stance might be, this tiny portion of chapter 20 on solitude and silence speaks well to all.

> Seek a convenient time to retire into thyself, and meditate often on God's loving kindnesses. Meddle not with strange writings; but read such things as may rather yield compunction to thy heart, than occupation to thy head. If thou wilt withdraw thyself from speaking vainly, and from gadding idly, as also listening to novelties and rumors, thou shalt find leisure enough and suitable for meditation on good things.[4]

Entering into a right relationship with our deepest selves is an entry into wonderment and astonishment. A transformed view of the world opens our understanding to see that, even though there are dark and dangerous sights, there is much that is beautiful; there are also potentially life changing possibilities that will re-establish life as productive and creative, pushing out hopelessness and apathy.

---

4. Thomas á Kempis, *Imitation of Christ*, 60.

3.4. Music/Painting

Music is available to all in a multitude of formulations. It ranges from hip-hop to high opera. At both ends of this spectrum, and in every place in between, people are moved by what they hear. Years ago, as a minister in a country town, I took a group of young people to another town to join with the district youth at a rock and roll night. Held in a show ground pavilion, the music was so loud, and the noise generated by excited young people so intense, that it was almost a solid barrier to all conversation. The young people thought it was great. Music can lift a person's spirit to the stars, and awaken singing, dancing, laughter, and much more. My age was showing—I just wanted to go home.

Music touches all our senses. We hear not only with our ears, but also with our body. I remember attending a concert at Monash University many years ago. The orchestra was fine and the music inspiring. In one piece, a number of trombones had a major place, and the music from those massed trombones moved me to tears. Many of us, no doubt, can recall particular pieces that were moving or inspiring, that took hold of our senses and led them down a path not of our choosing, but nevertheless fulfilling. Many who have lost their memory, and who have virtually no ability to communicate with others, have been known to come out of their lethargy to stand and dance to music. For some, when the music is a song they knew when young, their memory is awakened. Many of the pieces that I have listened to have left me within a quiet space, and some of those pieces have awakened many memories for me. In the noise that constantly surrounds us, music can quieten.

O'Donohue reminds us that in the noisy world silence is a gift that enables us to hear differently: "Give yourself the opportunity of silence and begin to develop your listening in order to hear deep within yourself the music of your own spirit."[1] Silence is not something we get a lot of; it is frequently not something that people want to hear. Some are afraid of the silence. The music of our own spirit can frighten, and many maintain activity and inner noise to avoid hearing that internal music, which is at times discordant.

There is a classic story in the Hebrew scriptures that claims silence as a most appropriate way to be in touch with the spirit. Elijah was a prophet, but after a climactic episode with the priests of Ba'al he ran away in fear for his life. He finally ended up on the "Holy Mountain." While hiding in a cave, he meets God in this way: "Now there was a great wind, so strong that it was splitting mountains and breaking rocks before the LORD, but the LORD was not in the wind; and after the wind an earthquake, but the LORD was not in the earthquake; and after the earthquake a fire, but the LORD was not in the fire; and after the fire a sound of sheer silence" (1 Kgs 19:11–12). It is then that Elijah leaves the cave, and it is then that he hears God. I imagine that the conversation, after all that turmoil, was music in Elijah's ears. O'Donohue continues:

> Music is after all the most perfect sound to meet the silence. When you really listen to music, you begin to hear the beautiful way it constellates and textures the silence, how it brings out the hidden mystery of silence. The gentle membrane where sound meets silence becomes deftly audible.[2]

The stirring music of Japanese drummers, or the large bell in a Buddhist temple, with its sonorous note, speak of a world rich in meaning. The great films that we see on the big screen and on our TVs are interlaced with music. The music becomes the thread that holds the film together. Tuned to drama, or comedy, or love, the music engages our senses as much as the visual presentation. In years gone by, silent movies always had a live musician to play along and follow the progress of the film. In the days when men went into battle with swords and pikestaffs, mounted on horses or on foot, they were stirred by bugle calls and drum beats. These were the music of battle.

Music, whether for dancing, or battle, or quietness, conjures for us the presence of spirit. We may find the spirit taking us by the hand and inviting

---

1. O'Donohue, *Anam Cara*, 99.
2. Ibid., 99–100.

3.4. Music/Painting

us to dance. We may also find the spirit taking us by the hand and inviting us to sing. Some of you may remember at the movies the occasional short film with the bouncing ball—"follow the bouncing ball." We may find the spirit leading us into quiet moments of reflection. Music does not invite us to think or reason, but to enter, maybe finding in its company a dancing God. There is clearly a spiritual element in music that takes hold of heart and mind and holds us fast.

In the Hebrew scriptures, with the stories of the Israelites and their God, there are many references to music, covering a range of human emotions. When the ark of the covenant, a fundamental ikon of the covenant between the Jews and their God, having been captured and then restored, was returned to the temple, "David danced before the Lord with all his might.... David and all the house of Israel brought up the ark of the Lord with shouting, and with the sound of the trumpet" (2 Sam 6:14–15). At another time in Israel's history, the land was conquered and people taken away to Babylon as prisoners. The psalmist laments, "By the rivers of Babylon—there we sat down and there we wept.... On the willows there we hung up our harps.... How could we sing the Lord's song in a foreign land?" (Ps 137:1–2, 4).

In our day also, people dance with all their might to the tune of jazz and rock bands, and perhaps a little more sedately to quieter music. When our mood is sad or somber, we turn to music that reflects our mood. I and others have wept at times on listening to music that enveloped and caressed the sadness. Through the centuries music has always been part of life. Its style may change, but in every age music has awakened something of the deeper spiritual urges that hover deep within.

I attended a Leonard Cohen concert and was entranced by all that was presented. Voice, music, words—it could be described as a complete package. It held my attention for hours, as it did for all the others in whose company I sat and listened. Music sets the nerve endings in our body tingling. Reacting to what we hear may result in a desire to dance, evoking sensual, or energetic, or happy movement. The music may evoke memories of events long forgotten, with tears of sadness or tears of joy.

Paintings have a similar effect. Many have the power to draw us into the picture and find there excitement, quiet space, or perhaps a sense of belonging. Tiny paintings of great beauty, large paintings packed with action and people, and much in between all have an effect on the way we perceive life as it was, and as it might be. They frequently offer us a vision of a different time when life was less busy, but may also show us times when life was hard and cruel. Sitting in contemplation, we may be invited by the picture to enter, and participate in the action. I have sat in the National Gallery in London and been drawn in to the magnificent paintings on display there.

Paintings may present us with colors that engage us, and at times transport us into a different way of viewing the world. Paintings frequently portray the artist's view of a spiritual world. In Orthodox churches, ikons have a most important place in drawing people towards God. In the times when people could not read, pictures in churches, depicting scenes from Scripture, became their books. They may at times have been rather fanciful, but they served a most important part in the faith life of ordinary people.

The visual images in paintings draw us into the picture, into some understanding of what the artist hopes we will see, allowing us to share for a moment the life of those portrayed. From a quiet rural scene to bitter fighting, and beyond into the myths of ages, we can pick our way through the action without danger to ourselves, and without disturbing the action. It can, however, speak to our spirit, stirring emotions, awakening desires, leaving us wrapped in our feelings, at times with a sense of contentment.

The art of the painter and the composer is such as to connect the viewer and hearer with a spectrum of life beyond everyday experience. The picture on our wall claims our eye from time to time and invites contemplation. Pictures can become a focus for meditation, and engage us in whatever they are depicting. They can become words in our mind that speak to us of fun and fancy, but also of the spirit of the divine, and make pathways visible along which we can walk or run as we wish. On those pathways, as we breathe, so we find the spirit accompanying us.

3.5. Imagination

IN THE BUSYNESS OF our world, with its mobile phones, pads, and computers, life has become so absorbed in activity that much passes us by. There appears to be no time to pause and be still. Competition for business, position, and power are pervasive and life takes on the form of a race. It is true that concentration and focus are important in the directions our life takes. It is also true that we need to stop running from time to time and consider what else might be important for life.

Life needs time to wander, to step aside and stand awhile. Pausing for a time provides opportunity to look around and take in the sights and sounds neglected when in a hurry. In public gardens in the spring, trees claim our attention with their new dress; flowers bloom, and among the trees and bushes birds and small animals may be recognized. In the autumn colours change again, and some areas of the world excel in the yellows, reds, and browns they produce. In this time it is possible for the to drift here and there, catching ideas, considering possibilities. In this time of stepping aside and wandering there is opportunity to soar, and look at the larger picture. In this time lies new ideas, images of possibility, and creative thinking. In this time we may ponder on all these matters that occur to us, and find an ability to take off in life and find new ways for living.

Imagination invites listeners to dream a lot, and apply the dreams to issues that are divisive in their application to people. The invitation of imagination is to consider the world as a unified whole rather than a series of countries with borders to enclose them, and keep others out. In imagination we may even reflect on a world in which wars, poverty, and want are no longer present, and multiple religious viewpoints are acceptable. In imagination we may also consider the value in people living the days.

PART THREE: SPIRITUALITY—RECIPE AND INGREDIENTS

The delightful book *Mister God, This Is Anna* offers, through the imagination in the dialogue shared by Fynn, the author, and Anna, the child, profound insights into the nature of the holy. Vernon Sproxton, in his introduction to the book, says that Fynn and Anna "put back the Ah! into that mixture of mess and marvel which makes the mystery of our mortal life."[1]

Searching for meaning, the primary focus of spiritual care, needs imagination if searchers are to plumb the mystery of our mortal life. When life stagnates among all the "if only's" and "I wish's" and "why me's," imagination can lift our sights and our spirits, and enable us to put the questions into appropriate perspective. Imagination does not solve our problems, but allows us to look beyond what is, to what might be.

Imagination is powerful. Imagination allows us, in our minds, to range far and wide, taking in every aspect of life, even recognizing possibilities for solutions to problems. Imagination, however, can become problematic if we decide not to return from our imagined world. Reality needs always to be an anchor in our lives. With this secured, imaginative travels can become catalysts for exploring new ways in which reality may be enhanced. Because we control our imagination, life is not threatened.

Imagination can become a pooling of ideas in the hope and expectation that workable options will occur. Imaginative thinking allows us to roam freely in the consideration of many options—a prelude to more adequate decision making. Imagination is its own reality, but needs always to be grounded in the possible. We are reminded of the imaginative thinking and dreaming that led finally to people literally being able to soar, and the excitement of seeing a flying machine that knew no bounds.

Imagination has played a large part in space travel, both for entertainment and for reality. For centuries people have looked to the sky and wondered. Imagination has frequently worked overtime, and we are all aware of the films produced with weird and wonderful beings living on weird and wonderful planets. The adventures of the Star Trek team and the saga of Star Wars have captured the imagination of millions. Imagination has become reality in the launching of people to the moon and satellites to explore the universe. Pluto, the remotest planet in our solar system, has been photographed. We are able now, from the comfort of our home, to view pictures of this distant place.

In more recent times, much that impacts life has been discovered: new treatments and medicines, some of which have become cures or

---

1. In Fynn, *Mister God, This Is Anna*, 12.

3.5. Imagination

preventatives in life threatening illness; new devices that enhance human ability to see and hear and function appropriately; new ways for dealing with global problems; and beyond the earth, new visions of space and its potential. All of these had their beginnings in imagination.

Imagination can help us to think through happenings that are affecting us and find the why, how, and when. Much occurs in life with considerable effect on personal experiences of living. The fatalist says, "That's life." If, however, we are to establish our life as hopeful and creative, we need to take time to consider imaginatively why this or that happening is so. From imagination we may find ways to meet our experiences head on, and incorporate them into our lives as enhancements.

There are times when we speak of another as having a vivid imagination. Mostly we are suggesting that they are considering something that could be labeled unworkable—perhaps outrageous, perhaps too difficult to consider. Saying "You are just imagining that" carries the sense of one being unrealistic. Clearly a variety of meanings may be attached to imagination. Nevertheless, it is also clear that imagination plays an important part in the development and expression of life events.

Yet another expression of imagination may be recognized in the idea of the *mind's eye*. In the teachings of the Tao, the notion of the *third eye* is given some prominence.[2] While this may not be precisely the same as imagination, there are some close links. The third eye is the ability to see what might be. In other words, the third eye is our ability to see beyond the potential. It is a sense, and it can be developed to be more refined and accurate than only being a hunch. The third eye is a natural part of every person, but it is a *meta-organ*. It consists of all the senses and mind working together as a larger, more powerful sensory organ.

In what way, therefore, we may ask, does imagination mesh with spirituality? Spirituality, like imagination, contains the ability to soar. Spirituality becomes an enabler whereby one may encounter spirit within, but also spirit revealed in responses to experiences of life beyond the everyday. In the context of spirituality, one may recognize sacredness in the lives of others, in natural phenomena, and in an indefinable sense of presence.

Spirituality, painted with a broad brush, depicts a canvas on which we find a host of images ranging from memories of good times, of friends, and of lovers, to reflections on relations between nations, war, peace, and

---

2. See http://personaltao.com/teachings/shamanic/about-visions/what-is-the-third-eye/.

justice, images of what might be, interspersed with images of what can be, and other images of things that may never be. Images of the sacred can also be found, couched in the ways with which we are familiar. This canvas of spirituality is imagination in action.

I have a sense that in the early days of the church, in its settling down into the organization of truth, imagination did not play a major role. The developing of a theological framework for the new religious way flowing from the life of Jesus was a serious task, as they sought to define and establish correct understanding in the developing and burgeoning church. Imagination, however, is important in our pondering about the nature of the holy. How else can it be done when we consider that God is an unknown, and that image carries many possibilities? This is not to say that imagination should spill over into fantasy. It needs to be grounded in thought and research as much as that can be possible.

Traditionally carrying messages of peace, compassion, prosperity, or happiness, prayer flags are a rich part of Tibetan Buddhist culture. Married to the biblical creation story, Buddhist prayer flags may be considered as caressed by the wind, which then carries their prayers into every corner of the world. We have noted elsewhere that the word for "breath" in Hebrew also has links to wind and spirit. We might therefore say that the spirit collects and distributes the prayers of all, and all may feel the breath of God as life and hope, even when expected answers are not forthcoming. The prayer flags can be imagined as a visible sign of the breath of God.

Thomas Moore writes of impoverished lives, and claims: "What is missing . . . is the penetrating enchantment of every experience that rises out of a world that is alive and that has deep and mysterious roots of power."[3] James Hillman writes of character:

> As we feel feelings, sense sensations, think thoughts, so we imagine images. We do not have to see them *literally*. We do not literally see the images in poems or the characters in novels, or even those in paintings. We "see" images with imagination, and that is how we see character, too.[4]

Stories, dreams, poetry, ballet, opera, musicals, drama, and comedy all require imagination for their appreciation. All provide a pathway along which we may travel with *third eye* vision.

3. Moore, *Care of the Soul*, 369.
4. Hillman, *Re-Enchantment of Everyday Life*, 183.

3.5. Imagination

Sarah Maitland shares a brief note written by Angela West, at the point of entry into her book:

> The sources of Christianity are largely without abstractions. We have a collection of stories, sayings, parables, letters and poems arising out of living experience. By sucking out—abstracting—the content Western theologians discard context and form as irrelevant and clothe them with the trappings of philosophical knowledge. All other forms of Christian truth are treated as second class. But the biblical texts are artful. The Bible's artfulness is our inspiration.[5]

Artfulness is concerned with story, and it is clear that the biblical narrative is overflowing with stories of a people and their God. The stories sweep across the centuries and tell of the growth of a nation from its beginnings as a family. Always the Divine is a central figure in the narrative. The stories do not depict historical facts; they speak rather of relationship.

Maitland writes in her introduction that she sees in herself a relationship between two parts: that of a feminist writer and that of a would-be theologian.

> Both these parts are convinced that, particularly at this critical moment of dissension and subjectivity, fiction, imagination and narrative have a vital role to play; that they can "refresh the parts that dialectic cannot reach" and are necessary to a fully human way of living in the material world.[6]

Janet Wood, in her introductory comment to *A Place at the Table*, has a pertinent point to make that reflects on the above quote. The context of the book has to do with the church's sacrament of the Last Supper, or Eucharist, and is written from a feminist viewpoint.

> Because of its centrality, the understanding that Jesus had invited only twelve men to share this time with him was important in the development of gender structure in Christian churches. It sealed the separation of women from one of the holiest points in Christian life and worship, and became a sign of other separations which broke the fellowship of the community of believers.[7]

---

5. In Maitland, *Angel and Me*, ix.
6. Ibid., xi–xii.
7. Fisher and Wood, *Place at the Table*, 13.

The lack of imagination in the development of the church opened the way for exclusion and dogmatic inflexibility.

In our time imagination is more than ever needed in the practice of religion. There is no place for exclusion and dogmatic inflexibility. Yet we find in churches—indeed, in all religious groups—areas of inflexibility that validate the labels. Many groups practice exclusion, seeking always to preserve their own belief practices. The stage is set for claim and counterclaim about elements of a faith stance. It could be seen as comical except that it is a serious problem that exacerbates divisions, and precludes imagination and creativity. Membership is frequently gauged by one's compliance with doctrine and acceptance of the boundaries.

In imagination, however, we can consider boundaries, most of which are lines drawn on a map, as no longer fixed in that way. Imagination allows us to flow, as it were, into the whole world, and recognize the beauty of human life. Wars and cruelties cannot prevent this inner journey, accompanied without doubt, by countless others in the world. From imagination we may emerge with determination to allow the spirit freedom, and find in the breaking down of barriers another insight into the meaning of spirituality.

3.6. Seeing into the Depths

IN EVERYDAY ACTIVITY OUR seeing is at a surface level. We go walking and our focus is on the path we are following, and our ability to walk that path. We don't spend a lot of time reflecting on the deeper issues that may be evident in a path. We don't spend a lot of time analyzing our walking style. Similarly, when driving our car the focus must be on the road, and our ability to negotiate any difficulties. This is important; we need to see where we are going. Focusing on the immediate visible clues is important for our safety, and for navigating our life. Navigating life, however, involves more than recognizing the road surface, or wind direction, or the setting of the tide. Always these things have a context, and the context has an influence on the settings, as well as on our reactions to those settings. The matters we observe and deal with in daily living invite us, as we become more aware, to enter a deeper, different interaction with them.

I am mindful of a tiny windswept island on the northwest corner of Bali. Around the jetty from which we made landfall could be seen a few metres of dead muddy coral reef. Putting on goggles and a snorkel, and slipping over the edge of this dead muddy reef. However, I was struck by the variety of fish, and the variety of their colours, as I looked under the surface and down into the deeper water at the reef's edge.

I once spent a couple of days in Venice, with its canals and tiny open squares—places of gathering. In one of those squares was a church, the wall of which was weather-beaten red brick with no adornments apart from a doorway. Walking through that doorway was entering in to sacred space, a place of light, and symbol, and quietness. From outside there was no indication of its contents and ambience.

Part Three: Spirituality—Recipe and Ingredients

Looking into the depths is not something we normally do. The fact of the matter is that in our daily there is frequently little time or opportunity. Crowded streets, and crowded buses and trains, do not allow for much more than a casual observation of others. We may notice what people are wearing or a particular habit or even a behavior. We may notice that many are talking on their phone, but rarely do we give a thought to what might lie behind the person we casually observe. It normally takes some specific event to cause us to consider what else we might find about the nature and circumstance of the one we casually notice.

Mary Marrocco shares from her experiences with underprivileged people in Toronto, Canada, a story about Frank:

> Frank is a thin, ragged man, always wearing a baseball cap and dirty jacket, who commonly eats with us. But not until I sat down with him at table, asked his name, and inquired what he had been doing with his day, did I learn that he spends most of his days visiting his mother in a chronic-care hospital just up the street, and so I learned to see in this tattered street man a loving and beloved son.[1]

Mary Marrocco, attuned to the needs of others, discovered a new understanding when she sat down to a meal with Frank, and changed the relationship.

As I look back at the above examples, it comes to me that the key understanding that emerges from each of them is awareness. To speak of spirituality is to speak of awareness—of spirit, of self, of others. Awareness is a precursor to understanding, and encapsulates a considerable number of feelings, attitudes, and perceptions. A brief examination of this will begin to reveal our own appreciation of the value in exploring that which is hidden below. Any surface of course has to rest on something in order to be what it is. What lies beneath takes on myriad forms. It may be the solid earth; it may be a deep sea. Always there has to be some form of foundation.

I expect you have all stood on a beach somewhere in the world and looked at the water. The surface may be calm or rough or stormy, but no matter how hard we look we will only see the surface. Much lurks beneath that surface, from hungry sharks to majestic whales to tiny organisms in their millions. To look under the surface is to look into a different world. So it is with our life when we take the time to look more closely into our daily experiences.

---

1. Marrocco, in Allen et al., *Prayer and Spirituality*, vol. 2, 411.

3.6. Seeing into the Depths

All of this needs to be securely grounded in the earth as the place in which our life begins, continues, and ends. We can lift off from the earth, but there are only two possible results. One is the surety that we must return if life is to continue and be meaningful. The second is being forever lost in space, drifting endlessly or being crunched by an asteroid. The earth is our home and we cannot escape by trying to run away. There is nowhere to run. If, therefore, we are to remain grounded, we need to increase our awareness of our environment, and learn to live consciously, carefully, and peacefully with all other occupants.

There is, of course, no blanket environment. Living is generally involved with a variety of environments, each of which has its own impact. One we can label the environment of place, and contains such facets as house, neighborhood, and state. Together these delineate the style of our living, with their rules, many of which are informal, and the norms that establish life in community. Community itself is made up of a host of relationships and interests, all of which enable people to develop their own niche in life with the security of friendship and family.

The environment of work has the additional potential of valuing skills, as well as providing income necessary to sustain life. Where we work is mostly in a place away from where we live. Through work many are able to find satisfaction in achieving results and in self-recognition. Work also can be dull and uninspiring, and for some a form of slavery. However we interact with work, it is an important and, I suggest, necessary environment.

Place and work both have an impact on the environment of relationship. In both circumstances we mix with people, and find a mixture of emotions in dealing with those we meet. Family, friends, and acquaintances all have a hand in our personal development. They all contribute to our journey towards awareness of self.

Awareness of self leads us to consider who we are in the deeper matrix of relationships that encompass us. This encourages the recognition that, while muscular strength may result from exercise and weaknesses from physical illness, there are, in the deep recesses of our being, responses to other's distress that explode into action in crises. Stories of rescue and heroism abound. Boundaries are stretched, and we find what we may become. Charles Birch writes of enriching life:

> The selfish person does not love himself too much, but too little. . . .
> He sees the rest of the world in terms of what use it can be to him.
> And he remains empty and frustrated. He sees his life as though it

were a sponge to soak up experiences instead of an outgoing urge to embrace the world. To love ourselves is to be open to influences that press in upon us from all sides that could transform us as the energy of the sun transforms a plant.[2]

Earlier we considered ourselves as bearing the image of God. If that is to be visible for others, we must follow pathways of care, compassion, and justice. Treading these pathways leads us to a true understanding of our self and an awareness that can rejoice in being. Awareness of others enables us to see the needs that people have, and see the ways—sometimes wrong—they take to meet those needs. Life is more than meeting needs, however, and we may recognize in others the infinite variety of physical shape, of mental ability, of emotional stability, of so much that marks our personality. In becoming more aware of others, we will also become even more aware that we belong with all these others. Despite beliefs and cultures, we all carry the potential to live justly and peaceably.

Awareness of the spirit takes us into a different world. Mindfulness of the spirit takes us into a dimension in which the sacred is both beyond and within us. Seeing into the depths, finding awareness, opens possibilities for seeing the world in a new way. I have already written of the world as a living organism, and our recognition of this must turn our hearts and minds to ways in which we can care for this living body.

We find, however, as we listen to business and government officials, and hear their views expressed on radio and television, that preservation is considered less important than exploitation. Governments and business speak of the value of exploration and extraction of minerals in the development of the country. One might consider, however, that government interest is more attuned to revenue from taxes, while business interest finds profits to be most desirable. The whole matter becomes economic—a surface mentality—and the losses in the degradation of land and the death of vegetation and animals are often reckoned as a necessary price to pay for economic gains.

Those who study the universe invite us by example to gaze into the depths as they claim that the creative processes continuing in the earth are in some way linked to the same processes continuing in the universe. As this is being written, we are privileged to witness the progress of a satellite as it skips past Pluto, a planet at the edge of our solar system, sending clear and revealing pictures of the planet back to us on earth. The data collected

2. Birch, *On Purpose*, 10.

3.6. Seeing into the Depths

becomes another small clue to answer the difficult questions about origins, the universe, our solar system, our earth. Theories abound, all of which may contain truth. Just as surely, it is claimed that more earths are contained in the whole. Another earth has only now been discovered, 1400 light years away. It is gauged to have many similarities with our own.

Religious belief contains the belief that the first cause is from the hand of spiritual forces. Many names are attached, but are essentially the same: "In the beginning God . . ." Religious belief needs to be recognized for what it is—belief. Belief awakens consciousness to the biblical story in which great care was exercised in the creation of the world. It is, however, not a matter of either/or, but of both/and. If we look carefully into the depths we will discern the great wonders of a universe that is beyond comprehension, within which we have a place of importance and life. If we look carefully into the depths we will discern beliefs that speak of wonders, though in a very different way. On the one hand we may look and see, on the other we may not see, but may find some sense of belonging within a life that discerns spirit presence.

It is clear from these few pages that there is much below the surface of living, revealing an array of facets that are knitted together in a variety of ways. These are not static; they are constantly in flexible relationship. Lives are influenced in many ways, and we continually rework, as it were, the forms that provide information about who we are. This reworking also invites us to consider the idea of spirit, and what this might hold for us as a way towards meaning.

Spirit presence becomes visible in individual awareness rather than in some collective awareness. As individual understandings meet, they establish the possibility that each can lead to wider understanding. The editor of *A Chorus of Wisdom* writes in her introductory comments:

> To me, spiritual living is living with the awareness that I'm part of something far greater. It is called by many names in many different disciplines. Some call it God, intelligence, universal energy, nonlocal mind, Spirit, consciousness or pure awareness. The Kabbalah says it is no–thing, and so can't be called anything at all. Quantum physics calls it the field out of which the entire universe is created. Eastern mysticism calls it *chi* or *prana*. It can also be called Life Force. It's the core essence we hear in the silence of our own hearts.[3]

---

3. Dubitsky, *Chorus of Wisdom*, 12.

Part Three: Spirituality—Recipe and Ingredients

The chorus of wisdom is indeed the chorus of respondents who have experienced some sense of spirit presence in their lives. As individuals they have looked well below the surface of life, and in chorus proclaimed their experience.

Seeing into the depths focuses our attention on matters deeper than life as it is mostly lived, and makes us sensible to possibilities that lie beyond our immediate understanding, but nevertheless affect our life in their impact on our heart and mind. In the book *A Magic Monastery* we read: "I walked up to an old, old monk and asked him, 'What is the audacity of humility?' This man had never met me before, but do you know what his answer was? 'To be the first to say I love you.'"[4] To be the first to say this is to become exposed to the possibility of rejection and even ridicule.

Expressions of love require some inner searching and courage in the uttering, particularly if an answer is expected and not provided, or the declaration is rejected out of hand. Both of these are possibilities. To say "I love you" and not expect an answer is yet a further step into vulnerability. The declaration from the depths of one's feelings may be tossed aside. Looking into the depths, whether the depths of the universe, the depths of the sea, or the depths of our life, is fraught with many risks, but also contains the promise of new vistas that are life enhancing.

4. Theophane the Monk, *Magic Monastery*, 68.

3.7. Darkness Covered the Earth

"In the beginning when God created the heavens and the earth, the earth was a formless void and darkness covered the face of the deep, while a wind from God swept over the face of the waters" (Gen 1:1–2). So begins the Hebrew creation story, and God moves to make the changes necessary for sustained and permanent life. Darkness has begun to be lifted.

The twentieth century, however, which recently closed, was a century of considerable darkness. Maria Harris, in *Proclaim Jubilee!*, writes of this century:

> Two world wars testify, one ending in an armistice that did not hold, the other ending with unbelievable carnage in the firebombing of civilian populations such as those of Dresden and Hamburg and the destruction not only of the cities but of the people of Hiroshima and Nagasaki. Bosnia testifies, Kuwait testifies, Rwanda testifies. Vietnam testifies too, (. . .). A core of unbelievable horror, the Holocaust of European Jews, remains a fissure of evil unfathomable, inexpressible, incomprehensible, scarring the face of the twentieth century.[1]

Victor Frankl also writes movingly of the deep darkness that permeated the lives of prisoners in Auschwitz during the time of the Second World War.[2] The darkness affected people in various ways. Those who were the enforcers of rule were cruel and callous, and relished their task as enforcers. There was no pity and no compassion in the darkness that controlled them. The darkness devolved onto prisoners through their ongoing suffering, which seeped into the very core of their being.

---

1. Harris, *Proclaim Jubilee!*, 11.
2. Frankl, *Man's Search for Meaning*.

Part Three: Spirituality—Recipe and Ingredients

Very early in the biblical creation story we are told that "darkness covered the face of the deep, while a wind from God swept over the face of the waters." The spirit or breath of God flows across the surface, carrying life, and creation begins and continues. Creation continues today in an ever-changing process, including the evolution of people and the multitude of religious systems in which they live. Creation is not about preparing the world for Christians (or any other religious group) to live in and take over; it is about gathering together by the spirit all people, who despite their differences will be able to live creatively together.

The history of Christianity is thought of, in the church, as reaching back through its Jewish ancestry to the very beginnings of creation—if not taking it all literally, taking it as stating a truth. The beginning stories include one that describes the advent of human beings. Represented by Adam and Eve, they are located in the story in the Garden of Eden. There they are made welcome as friends of God. Their place in that relationship requires a degree of obedience towards God, and their failure to live up to this requirement finds them expelled from the garden. From this story, accepted in the church as a reality in the creation saga, a doctrine of original sin eventually formed, and was refined over the years by the church. Belief, in the church, acknowledges sin as a fact, but seeks nevertheless to claim relationship with God as a forgiven member of what is named as the *body of Christ*.

The church, however, while describing itself as a personification of Christ, the light of the world, has in many instances been responsible for great darkness in the world—in recent times, the exploitation and abuse of children. This has continued until our day, and no doubt the church would have continued to cover evil if it had not been revealed.

Recent history bears witness to many violent conflicts that have their foundations in tribal associations and jealousies. These have been dominant in Africa among groups of people whose traditional land boundaries were overridden in colonial times by land-hungry foreign powers. Land, kinship, power, wealth, poverty, and desire for a better life have all been triggers for conflict, at times breaking out into genocide.

Among these groups, religious expressions may contain, either overtly or as residual hurts and anger, a measure of distrust of colonial expressions that continue in the lives of many. In Australia, we lay claim to homogeneity in which there has been no need for tribal conflict. In fact, we have had our conflicts, minor though they may be against a global backdrop. We have been colonizers, and have like the colonizers of other places subjected the indigenous population to indignity and violence. C. D. Rowley has much to say about policy and practice within Australia. The following brief extract on Aboriginal inclusion in the general community points up something of the difficulty with frequently hidden community racism:

> One of the most interesting examples of the philosophy that all is well, that the Aboriginal is really struggling to be like whites, and that his squalor indicates his innate handicaps, with careful tuition offering the best hope for him, is that which looks at the town fringe as a "learning" situation—a stage where the family learns housekeeping before moving into town.[3]

Rowley's work is forty years old, but the comments it contains are still true today. There are still fringe dwellers in many towns. People have tended to forget all this, preferring a more rosy religious description. As lovers of the good life, we have ignored much of the underbelly of Australia in order to enjoy our pleasures. Thus we appear as contributing to darkness.

Darkness is truly the cloak that covers all manner of wrong. As frequently reported in our media, social fracturing is far more common in the night than it is during the day. Paradoxically, night and day are essential for our well-being. Healthy living requires both, and both together constitute a day. In this whole day, sleep and activity become partners in our life. Together they provide light by which we can work and play, relief from the glare of the sun, and a time for quiet reflection, sleep, and regeneration. Together they are a vital part of life.

Fear of darkness can circumscribe our life to such an extent that we become unable to function adequately as a person. Limits are established, and fear imposes these on our days. We become afraid of our own shadow. Ursula Le Guin's book *The Earthsea Trilogy* is a story of a wizard with the secret name Ged, who, when young, as a result of playing with magic, awakened a dark being that then pursued him throughout his days. Ged, considering that this shadowy being was bent on destroying him, spends a lot of energy in seeking to avoid this creature. There comes a time, however, when he must face his pursuer. He finds himself face to face with darkness, which crawls towards him.

> Still it came forward, lifting up to him a blind unformed snout without lips or ears or eyes. As they came right together it became

---

3. Rowley, *Outcastes in White Australia*, 209.

> utterly black in the white mage-radiance that burned about it, and it heaved itself upright. In silence, man and shadow met face to face, and stopped. Aloud and clearly, breaking that old silence, Ged spoke the shadow's name, and in the same moment the shadow spoke without lips or tongue, saying the same word: 'Ged'. And the two voices were one voice. Ged reached out his hands, dropping his staff, and took hold of his shadow, of the black self that reached out to him. Light and darkness met, and joined, and were one.[4]

Acknowledgement of our shadow, as essentially belonging to who we are, allows for living to be continually adjusted to enable connection with others and a sustained healthy community. As such, darkness and light become partners.

Darkness that becomes opaque, that obscures the patterns and values of life, takes us into incomprehensibility. In the midst of many gathered for prayer, terror lurks and becomes public in the bombing of innocents, and sectarian war. In the midst of hymns, and gathered congregations, and claims of loving care for all, abuse and oppression lurk. They become public only when the perpetrators are forced to acknowledge the crimes of many individuals, along with complicity and cover up. Poor physical and mental health, demonizing spirituality, and failing to sustain wholeness open the door to wrongness. Such deep darkness is deeper than that which preceded creation and the emergence of light and life; deep darkness covers all visibility. The wrongness we experience in deep darkness is not a wrongness of the earth, but a wrongness in the lives of people. However we name this, wrongness becomes visible in people's lives through war, abuse, the exercise of power over others, and the genocide that flares from time to time. The wrongness is essentially a separation from the Spirit, and the loss of a vital element of life. We may be able to say, even this early in the twenty-first century, that primitive tribalism practiced in the name of God will be a continuing scar on the face of this century. This leads me to ask, has there ever been a year left unscarred by those who practice evil?

Falling into spirituality has been denied, and spirituality has been attached to teachings and physical demonstrations of glory, obscuring the image of God, and destroying rather than creating. Denial of darkness has not only paved the way for evil, but has left many in an unwholesome life. If, however, there is an *isness* in spirituality, the wholeness of God must consist in light and darkness. It all becomes a problem for people when there is an almost wholesale denial of darkness. There is, however, a considerable mix

---

4. Le Guin, *Earthsea Trilogy*, 164.

of faiths and cultures, along with a darker history, which must all be heeded if life is to be sustained.

Tacey writes of "a larger part of reality over which we have no control."[5] The larger reality includes the darker side of nature, and while we may have no control about this, we do need to recognize the whole picture. Having no control over the reality, however, does not mean that we cannot do something about the darker side of our nature. Seeking an answer to this question will allow for the possibility of recognizing that the darker side of life is nevertheless part of life. Acknowledging our own darker side is the beginning of a journey towards wholeness. In this we may consider the possibility of hope.

Tacey writes further: "We fall into relationship with a secret or mysterious other."[6] In this relationship we begin to recognize wholeness, and see ourselves and others as people who need to become interdependent so that all will live, and the darkness and the light will, as night and day, complement each other and bring us to true humanity. We will find our way into *being*. Falling into relationship with the sacred requires a new sense of the image of the divine, and a new understanding of hope, which, if only attached to a future event, is no hope now. It requires a renewal of our sensitivity to awe, that we might consider the awe-fullness of the earth and bow down before its wonders. It asks us to use our imagination, to think of what might be alongside our knowledge of what is.

The secret or mysterious other is discovered among all people, and in all places of the earth. The mysterious other is also discovered beyond the earth in the immensity of space. Even denial does not affect the reality, although the idea of reality is frequently a reason for denial. It is normal to be a "doubting Thomas," but we do need to put our decisions on hold.

In life generally, much that governs our living is in constant flux. I think that as this is true in everyday life, so it is true of the secret or mysterious other. Discovering some of the mysteries opens windows through which further mysteries may be observed. Always we can look into, and beyond, and discover more. The mysterious other, for Christians named as God, invites us to look below the surface of things to recognize the intimacy of relationship, and the courage needed to love. It invites us to venture into the dark places of the soul, to travel the dark journeys, and find the wholeness that is our inheritance. More than anything it requires that we be just, unprejudiced but determined that justice happens in the world.

5. Tacey, *Spirituality Revolution*, 143.
6. Ibid.

3.8. Justice

JUSTICE, THE EIGHTH AND, for this book, final aspect of spirituality, gathers together the actions of people, and places them under a spotlight for illumination. We have to concede that being spiritual requires one to be just. The just one looks to him- or herself and then seeks ways of spreading justice around. It all has to do with life in the world.

Walter Brueggemann, in his foreword to Maria Harris's *Proclaim Jubilee!*, writes:

> Justice is of course the core theme of Jubilee—except there is no "Of course" for Harris. The notion of justice begins here in spirituality, and spirituality comes to be "our way of being in the world in the light of the Mystery at the core of the universe; a mystery that some of us call God." This is about justice? Yes, about justice, because justice is not an extra or special ad hoc agenda but rather a steady way of being in the world.[1]

A steady way of being in the world is significantly affected by the hiddenness of many things. Some matters probably deserve to be hidden, but a deeper examination takes us to the shadow, of which Jung made much in his analysis of human personality. The shadow side of being, when ignored or belittled, can leap into consideration in an event of wrongness. Wrongness can be related to Symes' comment, "knowing the back of the world."[2] This is where wrong develops, and grows and increases in stature. Wrong retreats, requires hiddenness, and leaves open the way to fear and confusion.

---

1. In Harris, *Proclaim Jubilee!*, xi.
2. Chesterton, *The Man Who Was Thursday*, 132.

3.8. Justice

There are many problems that beset societies, many of them hidden in the hurts that force people to the edge. Of all these I want to single out two, both of which are a great darkness. The first of these concerns the misuse of children. All around the world children are being sold into slavery. For some this means a life of unremitting toil, and for some a life of sexual servitude, hired out to satisfy the lusts of men from all walks of life, in every country of the world. There seems to be no end to the exploitation, nor is there any one group that stands out in the lust for gratification. Close to home we have discovered that members of churches, claiming relationship with God, and with the Christ, have been active perpetrators of injustice in outrageous and cruel ways. The treatment of children in church, and other institutional care, has been soiled by sexual abuse and harsh punishments carried out by those who would have claimed to be committed Christians. This has been exacerbated by the organizations' protection of offenders, and disbelief of the cries of the victims. One might suggest that both individuals and churches have abrogated their right to be considered exponents of the Christian way. The wounded children have been ignored. The wrongness continues.

The second may be found in the houses that line our streets. Domestic violence is rife in societies around the world—another hidden activity that results in bashings, discrimination, wounding, and death. Psychologically and spiritually, lives are trashed. The destruction of relationship is absolute. The core loss is a spiritual one, but this is not about religion or church. The loss settles at the very centre of our being, and we become disoriented and lost. In trashing lives we trash the spirit, the life giver.

Charles Colson, in *Justice That Restores*, writes of relational justice, and refers to a 1996 lecture by the Archbishop of Canterbury, who said:

> When a crime is committed, it causes damage to the relationship between the offender and the wider society, because the laws on which society relies have been breached, as well as between the offender and the victim. It also disturbs the relationship between the victim and the wider society, because the victim bears a disproportionate share of the hurt from an act that is supposed to be illegal.[3]

Colson's claim is that justice is not only about punishment of the offender, but needs also to be visible in the restoration of relationship. He links this to the Hebrew understanding of *shalom*. This, he says, "meant peace, but

---

3. Colson, *Justice That Restores*, 100.

not simply the absence of hostilities; it meant true harmony, that is, people living together in the right order that God intended."[4] From an interfaith perspective, we can speak of living in harmony for the sake of humanity.

Restorative justice is undoubtedly a most important activity in the maintenance of societal relationships. We cannot, however, only consider justice in relation to individual actions. Injustice is rife in the world. Nations war against nations, with a determination that battles must be won despite the consequences of destruction and loss of life. Nations also do battle with nature, and much of nature's resources are lost. Plant and animal life bears the brunt of exploitation, and many have become extinct. Still we continue to damage each other, and the earth on which we rely for life. "Where is justice to be found in all this?" and "What must then be done to restore some of the damage?" are questions that require an answer.

Finding a steady way of being in the world could be linked to toleration. George Carey writes of speaking to a friend about a lecture on toleration that he was to give. He was somewhat surprised when his friend suggested there were more important matters in the world than toleration. Carey writes: "I thought of Northern Ireland, of Serbs and Croats in Yugoslavia, of Israel, of the Shias and Kurds in Iraq, of the black majority in South Africa, of the Orthodox/Catholic tension in the Ukraine, and of Sikh/Hindu strife of India".[5] There is much we can add in the twenty or so years since Carey wrote, but his point remains valid. If we could be more tolerant of others, if we could be more accepting of beliefs and cultures, we would begin to find this way a steadying influence.

A blight has settled on the world, shriveling our attachment to the spiritual, and leaving us vulnerable to the predations of evil. Our breathing has lost its meaning; it has become ragged. We ingest drugs and alcohol, we breathe in sex and violence, and the raggedness of this blots out the wonder of the world. Hope is lost; our sense of the wonderful is lost; our creativity is lost; we can no longer be as little children—*the kingdom of heaven* is lost.

For justice to prevail we need to look into the other's face. It is by faces that we recognize and are recognized. Much can be gleaned from looking into the eyes of another. To look into another's eyes, however, is to become vulnerable. In a world in which justice is normal, vulnerability is a shared sense of our need for acceptance, and a recognition of respect and relationship.

4. Ibid., 101.
5. Carey, "Toleration," 3.

3.8. Justice

When only a back is seen, confusion may be the result. The world is complex, and the lives of people are complex with their many differences. Adding these to the natural disasters that beset us from time to time can exacerbate the confusion, which if allowed to fester can lead to violence and desperation. Two major triggers for confusion's development and growth are found amongst religious and political agendas, and we can all bear witness to the horrific possibilities that grow out of their corruption.

Injustice occurs in a multitude of forms, and throughout all levels of society. It is frequently, if not entirely, linked to the exercise of power and control. Injustice, even when recognized as such, is interpreted differently in different social contexts. The harsher the regime, the more likely we are to encounter areas of injustice, frequently visible in political impositions and despotism in areas of our world.

So much of the world is fragmented by war and sectarian violence, with cultures of fear developed to keep people subservient, and preserve the desired status quo of those in power. Hunger and want, exposure to heat and cold, and malnutrition and disease contribute to the wastage of human life. Injustice is rife, cruelty becomes endemic, and punishment is frequently summary execution.

We have been witness in our time to the back of the church, to the back of religious pronouncement, to the back of political promise and spin. As I have noted above, Chesterton through the words of Syme says, "We have only known the back of the world . . . everything is stooping and hiding a face. If we could only get round in front."[6] If justice is to prevail in our time, we need to get round in front.

Spirituality takes all this into account, but still seeks to take us into a steady being in the world, into a stability that recognizes the presence of spirit in the breaths that we take, on which we rely for life. Spirituality presents us with a definitive word, a prophetic word that defines justice and compels our attention: "He has told you, O mortal, what is good; and what does the LORD require of you but to do justice, and to love kindness, and to walk humbly with your God?" (Mic 6:8). And from the prophet Isaiah:

> Is not this the fast that I choose: to loose the bonds of injustice, to undo the thongs of the yoke, to let the oppressed go free, and to break every yoke? Is it not to share your bread with the hungry, and bring the homeless poor into your house; when you see the

---

6. Chesterton, *The Man Who Was Thursday*, 132.

> naked, to cover them, and not to hide yourself from your own kin?
> ... Then you shall call, and the Lord will answer ... (Isa 58:6–7, 9)

In some ways this last sentence is a call to reality. When so many suffer in the harshness of their life while many live in extravagant luxury, justice appears far away. Doing justice, loving kindness, and walking humbly in the footsteps of the Divine is in essence living a spiritual life. As we engage with a spiritual life, spirituality may be recognized in life, and also in a sense of spirit presence.

Spirituality, however, when defined as some vague attachment to a personal spirit or feeling, has lost its meaning and its way. Being spiritual is not something we share only with angels. It is always, for us, closely associated with our senses. It is who and what we are, but needs awareness in order to be taken in, welcomed, and sustained. It also needs a strong engagement with life.

We can recognize spirituality in the lives of people, but in catching these glimpses of spirituality we may need to think what else might be caught sight of in the corner of the eye, which we ignore at our peril. Many matters lurk in the corner of the eye, and must be attended to. These are the hidden and semi-hidden things that confuse our sight, and draw us away from the issues that confront us. Just as it is important to have a lateral view when driving our car, it is also important to be aware of the things that lurk in the corner of the eye. These are the seductive images that, although partly hidden, prey on our sensibilities, and lack of awareness. Seductive images have the potential to make a pathway towards injustice and evil.

Awareness opens another pathway, on which we might find a creative and fulfilling future in which justice will be received as the free gift it should be, and all find satisfaction and peace.

PART FOUR

Practicing the Art

We have engaged with interfaith spiritual care in three modules, recognizing that they all belong together, and lay the foundation for adequate and relevant spiritual care. We have explored the nature of the term "interfaith," its difficulties, and its contribution to elements that raise our awareness and enhance our understanding of difference. In spiritual care differences need to be bridged, and the series of chapters in this second part have been designed to draw us into some important measures for our practice. All engaging in spiritual care would claim some links with spirituality, and this third part has drawn together some important elements of spirituality to enhance our grasp of sacred beginnings.

Practicing an art involves, firstly, that we have an interest in the form we wish to practice. With this interest, we are constrained to take up the art of our choice. Some take music, some painting, some acting, some photography, and so on. The more pressing we feel the need to take up an art, the greater the effort in practicing, and developing some degree of expertise. Not everyone finds fame and recognition, and for some this signals the end of effort; but what matters more is the love of the art. The art of spiritual care, as with all art, needs from us a desire to understand spirit presence in our lives. With our discovery of meaningful living in our lives, it follows that we may wish to help others who also seek different ways for their lives. When this involves religious affiliations, we may find, as we are challenged by differences, some complications in our practice of the art.

Whatever the nature of our religious faith, we all run the risk of considering others to be of lesser value. This will always be the case if we fail to recognize that religious faith standpoints only come into play because they involve people. A faith standpoint stems from a claim made for the expression of that faith as a way forward in life. It serves as a convenient definition in the world of many faiths. Prior to articulating a standpoint, however, one must enter into a relationship, and discover the way in which this particular expression has emerged.

It is at this point that we need to recognize that others, following similar pathways, have arrived at different conclusions. Religious conclusions, however, are in reality always a kind of bus stop on the way; they can never be a final destination. Constantly we are faced with changes and differing possibilities. Also, people are not only religious, they are cultural animals, embracing cultural habits and norms that date back many years—some for hundreds of years. Despite religion and culture, the fact is that all are people, all suffer pain, all rejoice in the good, all bleed, all die. Even though we may look different as we do, speak differently as we do, and perhaps dress differently as we do, we are nevertheless all human.

It is clear, as we look back at the many facets of spiritual care we have explored, that the art of interfaith spiritual care is indeed an art. Art, be it painting, writing, drawing, or sculpting, knows no boundaries; each piece has its own value, and each piece offers creative dialogue possibilities. The art of human *being* also knows no boundaries. *Being* requires a recognition of individual value. *Being* incorporates all matters associated with human living. When pieces are discarded, or taken away, life becomes less whole. Practicing the art of spiritual care requires that first of all we recognize our commonality with others. This is fundamental for our understanding of *being*. We may be different, but we can never be separate from all others. All, at the deepest level of existence, are the same. We don't have to like everybody, but we do have to acknowledge that all carry value.

This matter of value is of profound importance for the living of an adequate life in interaction with others. Every day people are devalued and damaged by a host of events. These events lay bare attitudes that declare the inequalities that entrap people as they go about the business of living. From cowardly punches that leave another brain damaged or dead, road rage incidents with destructive outcomes, family violence, shootings, and stabbings, to political and religious extremism, every level of human interaction has its share of violence.

Dreadful deeds have shattered lives, and forced people into fleeing to preserve their life, and the life of family. They, in effect, have run for their lives. Thousands upon thousands have fought their way towards safety, and on the journey have been subjected to violence from each other, and from authorities trying to cope with the massive influx of human need. Many have been pawns in a vicious trade in human suffering. Many who have reached their journey's end have discovered a welcome that for some has been overwhelming.

A welcome, particularly one that invites strangers into a different land, speaks of value. It is a sign that people are not only of a particular group, but are also recognized as individuals whose value lies in their being a person, not in any religious or national attachment. It can be said also that many will never reach their journey's end.

The art of spiritual care has its beginning in such human need, and humans need relationship, acceptance, valuing, and justice. The whole ambience of spirituality is a relationship with the divine, in whatever way this is interpreted. Without doubt there is a link with mystery, and an acknowledgement of a different level of living. Life, enfolded in spirituality, offers hope and justice. It is from an understanding of spirit presence that the art of spiritual care can be observed and absorbed. It is from this that we recognize that practicing the art requires us to be hospitable. Hospitality itself is an art. Its base is acceptance, an interest in the needs of others, a desire to provide sustenance and safety, and an acknowledgement that meaning is attached to relationship; it is compassionate, and strongly grounded in authentic presence. This presence encompasses both the one offering hospitality and belief in a divine presence.

Spiritual care and its association with spirituality clearly resonates in its many facets with human need and experience. Whether people have travelled half the world to put violence behind them or they have simply come from around the corner, whether whole families or individuals, all need to find a hospitable solution. Any offer of hospitality is an offer of safety. Hospitality requires a certain outlook on life. Friendliness, warmth, and kindness are such that they encourage not only the practice but also the acceptance of hospitality—the sharing of space. Hospitality offered to a stranger is no easy thing, nor is it surprising that being offered hospitality by a stranger carries an element of uncertainty, and even fear. Refugees come from an unsafe place. The whole of their life is under threat, and the only solution is to leave behind all that was meaningful, all that gave substance to life, all that provided a safe place into which one could withdraw.

People also need basic necessities like food and water, and warmth and companionship. The refugees we are seeing at the moment have no habitat apart from bearing the name of the country from which they have fled. War, with its destructive force, has wiped out the homes of many. Violence among combatants has wiped out their security. Habitat has been left behind, and the future is most uncertain. How might they establish a different and secure environment? This is surely a function of compassion, and just as surely has a spiritual dimension. Meaning is found in relationship, and in the companionship of dialogue. When people engage with each other, and talk to each other, they begin to find each other. These are the beginnings of a safe habitat.

When people are uprooted from their familiar and normal surrounds, or have left as a result of war, with little they can call their own, habitat retreats into the distance, replaced by feelings of loss and lostness. When there is nothing left that might be recognized as a place in which to live, people begin to migrate in search of something with more security, and a greater possibility of permanency. Habitat includes places for socialization, places for work and play, and places for worship. When these are removed many are direly affected. A secure environment is of utmost importance in any search for meaning. This may range from the immediate security we feel in a dialogue with a trusted other, to living in a land where stability is maintained, and people's daily activities can be relied on to secure their life. Practicing the art of spiritual care offers the possibility of pathways to security.

Many in our society do not have a secure place. Domestic violence, substance abuse, and much more take away the security we may expect in our locale. Habitat that is insecure is reflected in the lives of those who sleep on the streets, who are forced to beg, whose health is compromised. These are frequently the strangers in our lives, the ones we tend to avoid. Whatever the stranger might look like, however, engaging in dialogue opens windows on life, through which we all may glimpse elements of each other that point to spirit presence.

Presence, of course, is essential in the provision of spiritual care; indeed of any kind of care that may be given. Presence is dependent to a large degree on understanding the other; in particular, understanding the nature of human need. Some of this stems from our own awareness of the place of the sacred in our lives. The dancing God scatters light and love; the difficulty for many is that life has become too hard. Spiritual care is a mutual dialogue in search of meaning, of particular importance for so many.

Presence has two platforms, one of which is our apprehension of the needs of another, and the other is our connection with that which gives meaning in our life. When we are truly present to another we will listen attentively to all that the other is sharing. As we listen we will hear the story being told, and the story not told. As one student revealed to me, "I have discovered that it is important to listen underneath the surface." In apprehending the story of another, we also need awareness of our own place in searching for meaning. Part of this is in our connection to the spirit and our claim on spirit presence. Understanding our own spiritual journey becomes very important in any dialogue with another about their attachment to spirituality.

When these are both in harmony we are able to stay with the one in need, and find ways to allow that need to be examined and worked through. Hadley Kifner, reflecting on his engagement with a caring group to facilitate growth, understanding, and healing, writes of letting others:

> be who they are . . . means caring for them fully, deeply, for no other reason except caring for each other is what we are created to do. We are not to save one another, fix each other, protect each other from pain and fear and despair; we are to love and abide together.[1]

"Caring for each other is what we are created to do." If we can accept this as part of our truth, we have begun to discover the meaning for our life. This discovery removes from us any sense of having to do something because we should as a result of our belief, or feeling good about our life because we have been able to assist another. Acknowledging our truth allows us to enter into the art of spiritual care rather than thinking of spiritual care as a task. The art will give us pleasure, and open even more pathways on which to travel with the spirit. It is supremely enhanced by attention to the platforms.

Presence is an investment of time and energy, arising from our perception of human need and a desire to engage with another in a venture of discovery. Some of this stems from our own awareness of the place of the sacred in our lives. If our God is a dancing God, then light rather than gloom will be scattered around; we will be known by this company that we

---

1. Kifner, "Dawn Watching," 389.

keep. An association that we might name as the "Company of the Dancing God" could be considered an enterprise with boldness, inventiveness, and creativity. In such an enterprise we may be clearly recognized as one whose place in the company is clearly linked to being present to others in time of need. Vulnerability is always possible, but this enables us to be clearly in touch with the vulnerability of the one to whom care is being offered.

Practicing the art of spiritual care may take us into unfamiliar places; it will make visible that which is sacred in our lives. Once we begin to explore meaning we will find consequences in discovering, that will almost certainly focus our attention on values that are other to our life. Practicing the art will most assuredly press us to explore the ingredients of spirituality. The ingredients we may claim to be equally valuable for all, but we may also discover that the mixing differs from religion to religion. Spirituality, however, takes us beyond the religions, which are frequently defined and regulated, to the mystery of existence. Thomas Moore writes of this mystery as *Care of the Soul*. But as he does so, he makes sure that we understand that this is not the generally accepted religious notion of soul. He writes: "Soul is not a thing, but a quality or a dimension of experiencing life and ourselves. It has to do with depth, value, relatedness, heart, and personal substance."[2] This is yet another expression of the art of spiritual care.

Music that draws us in is artful in its ability to play on our emotions. It can wreath us in tears. It can bring us to our feet with acclamation. A painting on the wall that draws the viewer into the scene is artful in its ability to lure and concentrate our attention. There is trickery of a meaningful kind as we respond to the music and the picture, and become absorbed in their message. We might, in a similar way, consider the spirit artful in the invitation and challenges that are revealed to us. I think we can legitimately state, therefore, that the artfulness of the spirit brushes the deep places of our life, awakening a sense of mystery. The artfulness of the spirit lies at the heart of the awe we feel in special moments, and of hope that is able to be expressed even when situations are dire. The artfulness of the spirit shows us depths and darkness, but does not leave us in despair. The artfulness of the spirit paints pictures for our imagination, unlocking visions of possibility, and images of the divine. The artfulness of the spirit reminds us of the importance of our place in humanity, and will not allow a denial.

In all of this we will discover the art of interfaith spiritual care.

---

2. Moore, *Care of the Soul*, 5.

Bibliography

Allen, Pauline, Raymond Canning, Lawrence Cross, and B. Janelle Caiger, eds. *Prayer and Spirituality in the Early Church*. Vol. 1. Everton Park, Queensland: Australian Catholic University, 1998.
Allen, Pauline, Wendy Mayer, and Lawrence Cross, eds. *Prayer and Spirituality in the Early Church*. Vol. 2. Everton Park, Queensland: Australian Catholic University, 1999.
Arnould, Jacques. *Darwin and Evolution: Interfaith Perspectives*. Adelaide: ATF Theology, 2010.
Arai, Tosh, and Wesley Ariarajah, eds. *Spirituality in Interfaith Dialogue*. Geneva: WCC, 1989.
Ata, Ibrahim Wade. *Us and Them: Muslim-Christian Relations and Cultural Harmony in Australia*. Bowen Hills: Australian Academic, 2006.
Avery, William O. "Towards an Understanding of Ministry of Presence." *Journal of Pastoral Care* 40/4 (December 1986) 342–53.
Bagir, Zainal Abindin. *Science and Religion in a Post-Colonial World: Interfaith Perspectives*. Adelaide: ATF, 2005.
Birch, Charles. *On Purpose: A New Way of Thinking for the New Millennium*. Sydney: New South Wales University Press, 1990.
Buber, Martin. *Between Man and Man*. Translated by Ronald Gregor Smith. London: Fontana, 1963.
Butler, Patricia Mary. *Reflections on Living While Dying*. Brisbane: Keun, 1997.
Cameron, Heather, Colin Hunter, Michael Kelly, and Randall Prior, eds. *Together in Ministry: Essays to Honour John Paver*. Parkville: Uniting Academic, 2009.
Carey, George. "Toleration." In *Many Mansions: Interfaith and Religious Tolerance*, edited by Dan Cohn-Sherbok. London: Bellew, 1992.
Carey, Lindsay B., and Ronald P. Daveron. "Interfaith Pastoral Care and the Role of the Health Care Chaplain." *Scottish Journal of Healthcare Chaplaincy* 11/1 (2008) 21–32.
Chesterton, G. K. *The Man Who Was Thursday*. Ware, UK: Wordsworth, 1995.
Chin Kung. *The Collected Works of Venerable Master Chin Kung*. Calamvale, Queensland: Amitable Buddhist Association of Queensland, 1999.
Cohn-Sherbok, Dan, ed. *Many Mansions: Interfaith and Religious Intolerance*. London: Bellew, 1992.
Colson, Charles. *Justice That Restores*. Leicester, UK: InterVarsity, 2000.

Bibliography

Como, Michael. "Listening to the Silence: Through Zen and Taizé." In *Spirituality in Interfaith Dialogue*, edited by Tosh Arai and Wesley Ariarajah, 3–7. Geneva: WCC, 1989.

Conze, Edward. *Buddhist Scriptures*. Middlesex, UK: Penguin, 1959.

Cornille, Catherine, ed. *Inter-Religious Dialogue*. Oxford: Wiley, 2013.

Cousins, Ewert. "The Nature of Faith in Interreligious Dialogue." In *Interfaith Spirituality*, edited by Philip Sheldrake, 32–41. Way Supplement 78. London: The Way, 1993.

Cracknell, Kenneth, ed. *Wilfred Cantwell Smith: A Reader*. Oxford: OneWorld, 2001.

Doehring, Carrie. "Teaching an Intercultural Approach to Spiritual Care." *Journal of Pastoral Theology* 22/2 (Winter 2012) 2.1–2.24.

Dubitsky, Sorah, ed. *A Chorus of Wisdom: Notes on Spiritual Living*. Berkeley, CA: Ulysses, 2005.

Dupré, Louis, Don E. Saliers, and John Meyendorff. eds. *Christian Spirituality: Post-Reformation and Modern*. London: SCM, 1990.

Edwards, Mark. *Image, Word and God in the Early Christian Centuries*. Farnham, UK: Ashgate, 2013.

Eliade, Mircea. *The Sacred and the Profane: The Nature of Religion*. New York: Harcourt Brace Jovanovich, 1959.

Engel, Sandy. "A Tale of Three Visits: The Gift of Silence." *Journal of Pastoral Care and Counselling* 63/1–2 (Spring/Summer 2009) 17.1–2.

Fisher, Judi, and Janet Wood, eds. *A Place at the Table: Women at the Last Supper*. Melbourne: JBCE, 1993.

Fitzgerald, Michael L., and John Borelli. *Interfaith Dialogue: A Catholic View*. London: SPCK, 2006.

Foster, Richard J., and James Bryan Smith, eds. *Devotional Classics*. San Francisco: HarperSanFrancisco, 1993.

Fox, Matthew. *Original Blessing: A Primer in Creation Spirituality*. Santa Fe: Bear & Co., 1983.

Freedman, David N., ed. *Eerdmans Dictionary of the Bible*. Grand Rapids: Eerdmans, 2000.

Fynn. *Mister God, This Is Anna*. London: Collins, 1974.

Green, Garrett. *Imagining God: Theology and the Religious Imagination*. Grand Rapids: Eerdmans, 1989.

Hammarskjold, Dag. *Markings*. Translated by Leif Sjöberg and W. H. Auden. London: Faber, 1964.

Harakas, Emily. *Through the Year with the Church Fathers*. Minneapolis: Light and Life, 1985.

Harris, Maria. *Proclaim Yubilee!: A Spirituality for the Twenty-First Century*. Louisville: Westminster John Knox, 1996.

Hebblethwaite, Brian. *The Christian Hope*. Rev. ed. Oxford: Oxford University Press, 2010.

Hedges, Paul. *Controversies in Interreligious Dialogue and the Theology of Religions*. London: SCM, 2010.

Hedley, Douglas. *Living Forms of the Imagination*. London: T. & T. Clark, 2008.

Hick, John, and Paul F. Knitter, eds. *The Myth of Christian Uniqueness*. London: SCM, 1988.

Hillman, James. *The Force of Character and the Lasting Life*. Sydney: Random House Australia, 1999.

Bibliography

Julian of Norwich. *Revelations of Divine Love.* Edited by Grace Harriet Warrack. 13th ed. London: Methuen, 1958.

Kearney, Richard, and James Taylor, eds. *Hosting the Stranger: Between Religions.* New York: Continuum. 2011.

Kelsey, Morton T. *The Other Side of Silence: A Guide to Christian Meditation.* New York: Paulist, 1976.

Kifner, Hadley. "Dawn Watching." *Journal of Pastoral Care and Counselling* 62/4 (Winter 2008) 387–89.

King, Carolyn M. *Habitat of Grace: Biology, Christianity and the Global Environmental Crisis.* Hindmarsh, South Australia: Australian Theological Forum, 2002.

Klostermaier, Klaus K. *A Survey of Hinduism.* Albany: State University of New York, 1994.

———. "Hindu-Christian Dialogue." In *Dictionary of the Ecumenical Movement*, edited by Nicholas Lossky et al., 519–21. Geneva: WCC, 2002.

Knight, David. *Science and Spirituality: The Volatile Connection.* London: Routledge, 2004.

Knitter, Paul F. *No Other Name?: A Critical Survey of Christian Attitudes toward the World Religions.* London: SCM, 1985.

Koenig, Harrold G. *Spirituality in Patient Care: Why, How, When, and Where.* Philadelphia: Templeton Foundation, 2007.

Korab-Karpowicz, W. J. "Martin Heidegger (1889–1976)." *Internet Encyclopedia of Philosophy*, edited by James Fieser and Bradley Dowden. http://www.iep.utm.edu/heidegge/.

Koyama, Kosuke. *50 Meditations.* Belfast: Christian Journals Limited, 1975.

Kramer, Kenneth P. "Jesus, as a Jew, Would Never have Said That." *Journal of Ecumenical Studies* 47/4 (Fall 2012) 609–14.

Küng, Hans. *Christianity and the World Religions: Paths to Dialogue with Islam, Hinduism, and Buddhism.* Translated by Peter Heinegg. Garden City, NY: Doubleday, 1986.

Pui-Lan, Kwok. *Globalization, Gender, and Peacebuilding: The Future of Interfaith Dialogue.* 2011 Madeleva Lecture on Spirituality. Mahwah, NJ: Paulist, 2011.

Lebacqz, Karen, and Joseph D. Driskill. *Ethics and Spiritual Care.* Nashville: Abingdon, 2000.

Leeming, David Adams. *Mythology: The Voyage of the Hero.* 2nd ed. New York: Harper Collins, 1981.

Le Guin, Ursula. *The Earthsea Trilogy.* Harmondsworth, UK: Penguin, 1979.

Lipner, Julius. "The 'Inter' of Interfaith Spirituality." In *Interfaith Spirituality*, edited by Philip Sheldrake, 64–70. Way Supplement 78. London: The Way, 1993.

Little, William, H. W. Fowler, and Jessie Coulson, eds. *The Shorter Oxford English Dictionary on Historical Principles.* Rev. by C. T. Onions. 2 vols. Oxford: Clarendon, 1973.

Mabry, John R. *Noticing the Divine: An Introduction to Interfaith Spiritual Guidance.* Harrisburg, NY: Morehouse, 2006.

Macauley, Thomas Babington. *The Miscellaneous Writings and Speeches of Lord Macauley.* Edited by T. F. Ellis. London: Longmans, Green, 1860.

Mackenzie, Don, Ted Falcon, and Jamal Rahman. *Getting to the Heart of Interfaith: The Eye-Opening, Hope-Filled Friendship of a Pastor, a Rabbi and a Sheikh.* Woodstock, VT: Skylight Paths, 2011.

———. *Religion Gone Astray: What We Found at the Heart of Interfaith.* Woodstock, VT: Skylight Paths, 2011.

Macquarrie, John. *Martin Heidegger.* London: Lutterworth. 1968.

Bibliography

———. *Paths in Spirituality*. London: SCM, 1972.

Maitland, Sara. *Angel and Me*. London: Mowbray 1995.

Makins, Marion, ed. *Collins Concise Dictionary*. 3rd ed. Glasgow: HarperCollins, 1995.

Makranski, John. "The Awakening of Hospitality." In *Hosting the Stranger: Between Religions*, edited by Richard Kearney and James Taylor, 109-14. New York: Continuum, 2011.

Manji, Irshad. *The Trouble with Islam: A Muslim's Call for Reform in Her Faith*. Toronto: Random House, 2003.

Marty, Martin E. *When Faiths Collide*. Malden, MA: Blackwell, 2005.

McCarter, P. Kyle, Jr. "Abraham." In *Eerdmans Dictionary of the Bible*, edited by David N. Freedman et al., 8-10. Grand Rapids: Eerdmans, 2000.

McLeod, Frederick G. *The Image of God in the Antiochene Tradition*. Washington, DC: Catholic University of America Press, 1999.

Metzger, Bruce M., and Roland E. Murphy, eds. *The New Oxford Annotated Bible*. New Revised Standard Version. New York: Oxford University Press, 1991.

Mohrmann, Margaret E. *Medicine as Ministry: Reflections on Suffering, Ethics, and Hope*. Cleveland: Pilgrim, 1995.

Moore, Thomas. *Care of the Soul*. New York: Harper Perennial, 1994.

———. *The Re-Enchantment of Everyday Life*. Sydney: Hodder and Stoughton, 1996.

Muck, Terry C. "Theology of Religions after Knitter and Hick: Beyond the Paradigm." *Interpretation* 61/1 (2007) 7-22.

O'Donohue, John. *Anam Cara: Spritual Wisdom from the Celtic World*. London: Bantam, 1997.

———. *Conamara Blues*. London: Doubleday, 2000.

Parekh, Bhikhu. "The Concept of Interfaith Dialogue." In *Many Mansions: Interfaith and Religious Intolerance*, edited by Dan Cohn-Sherbok, 158-68. London: Bellew, 1992

Percy, Martyn. *The Ecclesial Canopy*. Burlington, VT: Ashgate, 2012.

Porter, Muriel. *Land of the Spirit?: The Australian Religious Experience*. Geneva: World Council of Churches, 1990.

Poston, Larry. *Islamic Da´Wah in the West: Muslim Missionary Activity and the Dynamics of Conversion to Islam*. New York: Oxford University Press, 1992.

Prothero, Stephen. *God Is Not One: The Eight Rival Religions that Run the World and Why Their Differences Matter*. New York: HarperOne, 2010.

Puchalski, Christina M., and Betty Ferrell. *Making Health Care Whole: Integrating Spirituality into Patient Care*. West Conshohocken, PA: Templeton, 2010.

Purnell, Douglas. *Conversation as Ministry*. Cleveland: Pilgrim, 2003.

Rahner, Karl. *Encounters with Silence*. Translated by James M. Demske. London: Burns and Oates, 1960.

Rowley, C. D. *Outcasts in White Australia: Aboriginal Policy and Practice*. Vol. 2. Canberra: Australian National University Press, 1971.

Ryken, Leland, James C. Wilhoit, and Tremper Longman III, eds. *Dictionary of Biblical Imagery*. Downers Grove, IL: InterVarsity, 1998.

Schipani, Daniel S., and Leah Dawn Bueckert, eds. *Interfaith Spiritual Care: Understandings and Practices*. Kitchener, ON: Pandora, 2009.

Sheldrake, Phillip, ed. *Interfaith Spirituality*. Way Supplement 78. London: The Way, 1993.

Shinn, Larry D. *Two Sacred Worlds: Experience and Structure in the World's Religions*. Nashville: Abingdon, 1977.

Bibliography

Smart, Ninian. *The Religious Experience of Mankind.* New York: Collins Fount, 1984. First published, New York: Scribner's, 1969.

Speck, Peter W. "Spiritual Care in Health Care." *Scottish Journal of Healthcare Chaplaincy* 7/1 (2004) 21–25.

Stevenson, A., ed. *Oxford Dictionary of English.* 3rd ed. Oxford: Oxford University Press, 2010.

Starhawk. *The Earth Path: Grounding Your Spirit in the Rhythms of Nature.* San Francisco: HarperSanFrancisco, 2004.

Stratford, W. "A Study in the Re-Articulation of Pastoral Care within a Framework of Plurality and Difference." PhD thesis, Griffith University, Brisbane, 2013.

———. *To Live Each Day: Stories by People with Cancer.* Melbourne: JBCE, 1995.

Swidler, Leonard. *The Meaning of Life at the Edge of the Third Millennium.* New York: Paulist, 1992.

Thangaraj, M. Thomas. "The Challenge of Religious Plurality." In *Plurality, Power, and Mission: Intercontextual Theological Explorations on the Role of Religion in the New Millennium*, edited by Philip Wickeri et al., 197–213. London: Council for World Mission, 2000.

Theophane the Monk. *Tales of a Magic Monastery.* New York: Crossroad, 1987.

Thomas à Kempis. *The Imitation of Christ.* Edited by Paul M. Bechtel. Chicago: Moody, 1980.

Uhlein, Gabriele. *Hildegard of Bingen.* Santa Fe, NM: Bear and Co., 1983.

Volf, Miroslav, Ghazi bin Muhammed, and Melissa Yarrington, eds. *A Common Word: Muslims and Christians on Loving God and Neighbor.* Grand Rapids: Eerdmans, 2010.

Ward, Frances, and Sarah Coakley, eds. *Fear and Friendship: Anglicans Engaging with Islam.* London: Continuum, 2012.

Webb, Karen S. "Pastoral Identity and the Ministry of Presence." *Journal of Pastoral Care* 44/1 (Spring 1990) 76–79.

Wickeri, Philip L., Janice K. Wickeri, and Damayanthi M. A. Niles., eds. *Plurality, Power, and Mission: Intercontextual Theological Explorations on the Role of Religion in the New Millenium.* London: Council for World Mission, 2000.

Wilfred, Felix. "Religions as Agents of Hope: Challenges for the New Millennium." In *Plurality, Power, and Mission: Intercontextual Theological Explorations on the Role of Religion in the New Millenium*, edited by Philip Wickeri et al., 43–82. London: Council for World Mission, 2000.

Wolterstorff, N. *Lament for a Son.* Grand Rapids: Eerdmans, 1987.

Wright, Stephen G., and Jean Sayre-Adams. *Sacred Space: Right Relationship and Spirituality in Health Care.* Edinburgh: Churchill Livingstone, 2000.

Made in the USA
Middletown, DE
27 November 2019